Medieval Mississippians

Medieval
Mississippians
The Cahokian World

Edited by Timothy R. Pauketat and Susan M. Alt

A School for Advanced Research Popular Archaeology Book

SAR
PRESS

School for Advanced Research Press
Santa Fe

School for Advanced Research Press
Post Office Box 2188
Santa Fe, New Mexico 87504-2188
www.sarpress.org

Managing Editor: Lisa Pacheco
Editorial Assistant: Ellen Goldberg
Designer and Production Manager: Cynthia Dyer
Manuscript Editor: Jane Kepp
Proofreader: Patricia Kot
Indexer: Ina Gravitz
Printed by Lifetouch through the Four Color Print Group

Library of Congress Cataloging-in-Publication Data
Medieval Mississippians : the Cahokian world / edited by Timothy R. Pauketat and Susan M. Alt.
pages cm. — (Popular archaeology)
Includes bibliographical references and index.
ISBN 978-1-938645-31-0 (cloth : alk. paper) — ISBN 978-1-938645-32-7 (pbk. : alk. paper)
1. Mississippian culture. 2. Cahokia Mounds State Historic Park (Ill.) 3. Indians of North America—Mississippi River Valley—
Antiquities. 4. Indians of North America—Middle West—Antiquities.
I. Pauketat, Timothy R., editor. II. Alt, Susan M., 1959–, editor. III. Title: Cahokian world.
E99.M6815M38 2014
977'.01—dc23
2014005389

Cover photograph: Detail of aerial view of the central, or "downtown," Cahokia precinct.
Photo by Ira Block, used with permission of the National Geographic Society.

*The School for Advanced Research (SAR) promotes the furthering of scholarship on—and public understanding of—human culture,
behavior, and evolution. SAR Press publishes cutting-edge scholarly and general-interest books that encourage critical thinking
and present new perspectives on topics of interest to all humans. Contributions by authors reflect their own opinions and viewpoints
and do not necessarily express the opinions of SAR Press.*

Contents

Color plates follow page 64.

Acknowledgments

We have enjoyed working with our colleagues and friends on this book. We especially want to thank James F. Brooks, former president and CEO of the School for Advanced Research, who supported the project throughout, and the staff of SAR Press, who made the book possible, particularly director Lynn Thompson Baca, managing editor Lisa Pacheco, and series editor Jane Kepp. Many more people behind the scenes, of course, help to bring a book like this to fruition. They include archaeologists, students, and American Indian authorities and consultants who worked on the projects that resulted in the interpretations and imagery presented here. Among these people, we would especially like to thank Chloris Lowe Jr., Chloris Lowe Sr., and Bill Quackenbush of the Ho-Chunk Nation; Rodney Steve of the Choctaw Nation; Carrie Wilson of the Quapaw Tribe; and Kirk Perry of the Chickasaw Nation.

Many other persons and institutions have allowed access to and reproduction of their images. Special thanks go to Stacy Allen, David Anderson, John Cornelison, John Doershuk, Thomas Emerson, Dale Henning, and William Iseminger and to the National Park Service, the Illinois State Archaeological Survey, the Iowa Office of the State Archaeologist, and Cahokia Mounds State Historic Site. Molly O'Halloran drew some of the maps, and Linda Alexander, Michael Farkas, Mera Hertel, Jeffrey Kruchten, and Michael Lewis produced other photographic and digital images. Glenn Baker, Chloris Lowe Sr., Bernard Perley, and Herb Roe produced drawings and watercolors for the book. The artwork of Theodor de Bry, Michael Hampshire, Jacques Le Moyne, Al Meyer, Lloyd K. Townsend, and John White is also featured here.

Funding for the archaeological projects described in the book and support for the production of text and imagery have come from the Illinois Department of Transportation, the Illinois State Archaeological Survey, the Historical Society of Boston's Research and Innovation in Human Affairs Program, the National Science Foundation, the National Geographic Society, the Arkansas Archeological Survey, and the Center for Advanced Spatial Technologies at the University of Arkansas. Finally, we would like to acknowledge the Amerind Foundation, in Dragoon, Arizona, and its director, John Ware, for support in the form of visiting scholar appointments in the fall of 2012, during which time we pulled chunks of this volume together.

Places to Visit in the Cahokian World and Beyond

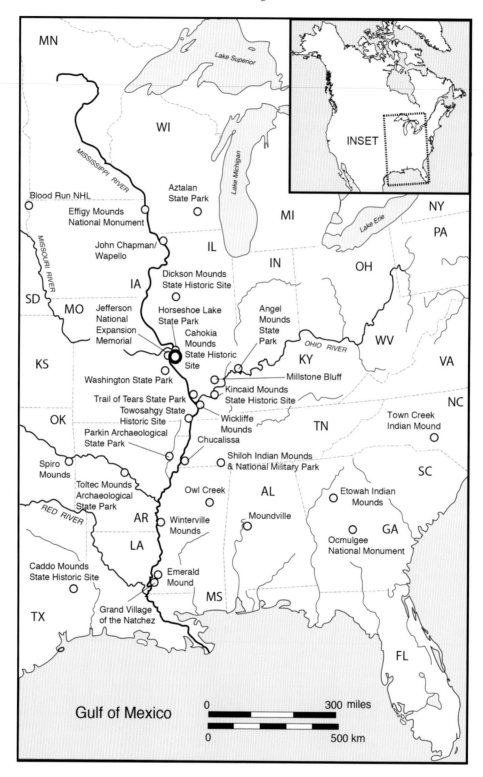

Map 1. Publicly accessible archaeological sites of the medieval Mississippian world.

Angel Mounds State Park. Angel Mounds, on the Ohio River near Evansville, Indiana, was an impressive early Mississippian walled town enclosing one hundred acres and a dozen platform mounds. Built shortly after 1050 CE, Angel housed perhaps a thousand people until about 1450. Museum exhibits and reconstructions. Admission fee. http://www.indianamuseum.org/explore/angel-mounds.

Aztalan State Park. This is Wisconsin's premier archaeological site, a large Late Woodland village and later a medieval Mississippian outpost established by or with the aid of Cahokians just after 1050 and inhabited through the 1200s. Two prominent, flat-topped, pyramidal mounds sit within a bastioned palisade wall. One row of mounds may be seen, beginning at an unofficial visitor center. The park sits at the edge of Aztalan, Wisconsin, on the east side of Jefferson County Highway Q, just south of County Highway B. Vehicle admission fee. http://dnr.wi.gov/topic /parks/name/aztalan/.

Blood Run National Historical Landmark. This Oneota settlement and mound complex covers more than twelve hundred acres in western Iowa and eastern South Dakota. Visitors can view 50 of an original 275 mounds, one of which was a serpent effigy. The Oneota culture appears to have originated in Wisconsin in the late 1100s or 1200s, sparked by Late Woodland–Mississippian contacts. Historically, the Umoⁿhoⁿ (Omaha) people lived at Blood Run, but other peoples visited or lived with them, producing concentrations of as many as six thousand people. No formal visitor facilities. http://www.iowahistory.org/historic-sites/blood -run/site-history.html.

Caddo Mounds State Historic Site. Situated twenty-six miles west of present-day Nacogdoches, Texas, this southwesternmost Caddoan town was centered on two platform mounds and one burial mound, all founded around 800 CE and occupied into the 1200s. Visitor center. Admission fee. http://www.visitcaddomounds.com/index.aspx ?page=2.

Cahokia Mounds State Historic Site. Much of the heart of Cahokia is preserved in this Illinois state park, a short drive east from St. Louis, Missouri. It includes Monks Mound, the Grand Plaza, Rattlesnake Causeway, and scores of earthen pyramids out of the original 120. Originally an impressive Late Woodland village, the site was converted around 1050 CE into a planned city of ten thousand or more people, encompassing two other precincts that cannot be visited today. A large interpretive center features artifacts and exhibits from the area. No admission fee but a suggested donation. Nearby are Horseshoe Lake State Park and Jefferson National Expansion Memorial. http://www.cahokiamounds.org.

Chucalissa and the C. H. Nash Museum. Around 1200 CE, Chucalissa, a Mississippian town with platform mounds, was established on an old town site in present-day Memphis, Tennessee. After a gap, a late Mississippian town thrived there, connected to peoples in the modern states of Mississippi, Kentucky, and Illinois. Museum exhibits and on-site reconstructions. Admission fee. http:// www.memphis.edu/chucalissa/.

Dickson Mounds State Historic Site. The Dickson Mounds Museum overlooks the colonial Cahokia-Mississippian site of Eveland in west-central Illinois. After Eveland was abandoned, around 1150, descendants living in Mississippian settlements nearby continued to use its cemetery for generations. The museum was built over and adjacent to the burial ground. No admission fee. http://www.museum.state.il.us/ismsites/dickson/ and http://www.experienceemiquon.com/content/ dickson-mounds-museum-2.

Effigy Mounds National Monument. Three miles north of Marquette, Iowa, are preserved more than two hundred effigy and conical mounds. These were the sacred burial and pilgrimage sites of Late Woodland peoples in one the most picturesque parts of the upper Mississippi River valley. Most immediately predate Cahokia's emergence and the spread of Mississippian cultures. Visitor center exhibits. Admission fee. http://www.nps.gov /efmo/index.htm.

Emerald Mound National Historic Landmark. Ten miles northeast of Natchez, Mississippi, this artificially sculpted hill is topped with two smaller pyramidal mounds. The surrounding town was occupied from around 1250 to 1600 by ancestors of the Natchez Indians. No admission fee. http://www.nps.gov/nr/travel/mounds/eme.htm.

Etowah Indian Mounds Historic Site. This fifty-four-acre town, now a Georgia state park near Cartersville, Georgia, boasted six earthen mounds, a plaza, and a defensive ditch, all dating between about 1100 and 1550. Etowah's central pyramid towers sixty-three feet above the rest of the site. On-site museum. Admission fee. http://www.gastateparks.org/EtowahMounds.

Grand Village of the Natchez Indians. Given the name Grand Village by French explorers, this place was the main town and administrative capital of the Natchez Indian people from 1682 to 1729. The archaeological park today covers 128 acres in Natchez, Mississippi. It features three earthen platforms and an interpretive center. No admission fee. http://mdah.state.ms.us/hprop/gvni.php.

Horseshoe Lake State Park. Within the boundaries of this park near Granite City, Illinois, is a small Cahokian town with a single platform mound, dating to 1050–1100 CE. The eroded, tree-covered mound overlooks a great bend in the old channel of the Mississippi River. Aquatic and bird life abounds in the park, which preserves many more Mississippian farmstead and village sites. No admission fee. http://dnr.state.il.us/Lands/landmgt/parks/R4/HORSESP.HTM.

Jefferson National Expansion Memorial. Situated in the heart of downtown St. Louis on the Mississippi River, this park lies just one-half mile south of Cahokia's St. Louis precinct. The Jefferson National Expansion Memorial includes the Gateway Arch and the Museum of Westward Expansion, where exhibits connect pre-Columbian indigenous cultures to the westward expansion of the United States. Admission fee. http://www.nps.gov/jeff/index.htm.

John Chapman archaeological site on the Wapello Land and Water Reserve. The John Chapman archaeological site, situated along the Apple River in northwestern Illinois, just south of Hanover, is part of a publicly accessible prairie preserve and park now owned by the Jo Daviess Conservation Foundation. This Mississippian village dated from 1050 to 1200 CE and was populated by local people under the influence of Cahokia. Many Late Woodland effigy mounds still line the banks of the Apple River and the bluff tops nearby; they are possibly what attracted Cahokians to this part of Illinois. No admission fee. http://www.isas.illinois.edu/illarchtoday/wapello.shtml and http://www.jdcf.org/wapello_land.aspx.

Kincaid Mounds State Historic Site. At this unimproved state historic site near Brookport, on the Ohio River in southernmost Illinois, an interpretive platform overlooks impressive pyramidal mounds covering 105 acres, with more on adjacent private property. This early, palisaded Mississippian town dated from the late 1000s to 1400. No admission fee. http://www.kincaidmounds.com.

Millstone Bluff Archaeological Site. Near the town of Robbs, Illinois, sits the beautifully preserved mesa-top site of a late Mississippian village and cemetery. Still visible are house depressions and petroglyphs that conveyed the residents' understanding of the cosmos. No admission fee. http://www.visitgolconda.com/hit-the-trails/millstone-bluff-archaeological-site/ and http://www.fs.usda.gov/recarea/shawnee/.

Moundville Archaeological Park. Moundville was a large Mississippian town on the Black Warrior River near present-day Tuscaloosa, Alabama. From the 1100s to 1300 it was the administrative capital of a territory encompassing lesser towns. At its peak, Moundville covered two hundred acres protected by a bastioned wooden palisade. Within the wall were twenty-six platform mounds, ceremonial and public buildings, and residences. Visitor center. No admission fee. http://moundville.ua.edu.

Ocmulgee National Monument. The Ocmulgee site, atop the Macon Plateau near Macon, Georgia, appears to have been an intrusive settlement of early Mississippians who settled in the midst of local Woodland tribes. The immigrants built residential mounds and earth lodges. Later Mississippian inhabitants followed what archaeologists call the Lamar culture. Visitor center. No admission fee. http://www.nps.gov/ocmu/index.htm.

Owl Creek Site. This Mississippian town, now in the Tombigbee National Forest southwest of Tupelo, Mississippi, included five platform mounds built around 1100–1200 CE. The largest stands seventeen feet high. No admission fee. http://www.nps.gov/nr/travel/mounds/owl.htm.

Parkin Archaeological State Park. A seventeen-acre Mississippian town lay along the St. Francois River at present-day Parkin, Arkansas, as early as the 1100s. A large platform mound still stands on the riverbank; many people believe it was the tumulus described by Hernando de Soto's chroniclers in 1541 when they visited a town the Native people called Casqui. Visitor center. No admission fee. http://www.arkansasstateparks.com/parkinarcheological/#.UTn_R6XwFUQ.

Shiloh Indian Mounds and National Military Park. The Civil War battle of Shiloh took place around a great Mississippian town, which from about 1050 to 1350 possessed seven earthen platforms and a wooden palisade. The southernmost mound is a ridge-top tumulus in which important people were buried. At the Tennessee River Museum in nearby Savannah, Tennessee, the famous Shiloh effigy pipe is on display. No admission fee. http://www.nps.gov/shil/mounds.htm.

Spiro Mounds. Located seven miles west of modern-day Spiro, Oklahoma, the indigenous Spiro settlement was a large Caddoan-Mississippian town. Living between the Great Plains, the Cahokian realm, and the Southeast, Spiroans exerted considerable influence over peoples of all three areas. Surreptitious looting in the 1930s, and later professional archaeological excavations, documented a great mortuary complex at Spiro that included cultural objects from all over the Mississippian world. Visitor center. Admission fee. http://www.okhistory.org/sites/spiromounds.

Toltec Mounds Archaeological State Park. The Toltec site, southeast of Little Rock, Arkansas, is one of the most impressive civic-ceremonial complexes in the lower Mississippi Valley. There, eighteen impressive flat-topped pyramids were surrounded by an earthen embankment some eight to ten feet high, only a portion of which can be seen today. Closely related to the Coles Creek culture to the south, the Plum Bayou people of Toltec built their town from 700 to 1050 CE and left it at the time of Cahokia's founding. Visitor center. No admission fee. http://www.arkansasstateparks.com/toltecmounds/#.UTngyqXwFUQ.

Town Creek Indian Mound. This southern Appalachian Mississippian town, near modern Mount Gilead, North Carolina, was occupied from the later 1100s to about 1450 and was the center of the Pee Dee culture. Its single platform mound can be seen today with a reconstructed pole-and-thatch building on top surrounded by a wooden palisade wall. Visitor center. No admission fee. http://www.nchistoricsites.org/town/.

Towosahgy State Historic Site. Near East Prairie, Missouri, this archaeological site was one of several densely populated, fortified Mississippian towns in southeastern Missouri that date from about 1200 to 1400 CE. The well-preserved earthen pyramids are interpreted through exhibit panels, and visitors can walk a trail through the mounds. No admission fee. http://mostateparks.com/park/towosahgy-state-historic-site.

Trail of Tears State Park. This Illinois park, near Jonesboro, preserves a piece of the Trail of Tears, the trace along which the US Army forcibly marched people of the Cherokee, Creek, and Chickasaw nations to reservations in Oklahoma Territory in 1838 and 1839. Bitter winter weather and starvation claimed hundreds of lives in makeshift camps near here. No admission fee.

http://dnr.state.il.us/lands/landmgt/parks/r5
/trltears.htm.

Washington State Park. Situated on the eastern edge of the Ozarks, a rugged, forested landscape frequented by Cahokian and other Mississippian peoples, this park near De Soto, Missouri, preserves a wide array of Mississippian-era rock-art petroglyphs. No admission fee. http://mostateparks.com/park/washington-state-park.

Wickliffe Mounds. From 1100 to 1350 CE, a small Mississippian town occupied the bluff top overlooking the Mississippi River near its confluence with the Ohio at present-day Wickliffe, Kentucky. A series of earthen mounds is situated around a central plaza. Welcome center, museum exhibits, gift shop, walking trail, picnic areas. Admission fee. http://parks.ky.gov/parks/historicsites/wickliffe-mounds/.

Winterville Mounds. This great Coles Creek and Mississippian center now in Greenville, Mississippi, dates from about 1000 to 1450. The large earthen pyramids were platforms for pole-and-thatch temples, elite houses, and other buildings. The site originally contained at least twenty-three mounds, twelve of which—including the fifty-five-foot-high Temple Mound—lie in the park. Visitor center. No admission fee. http://mdah.state.ms.us/hprop/winterville.php.

Map 2. Ancient cultural regions and indigenous tribes and nations of North America, from the 1600s through the 1800s, that were historically connected to the Cahokian world.

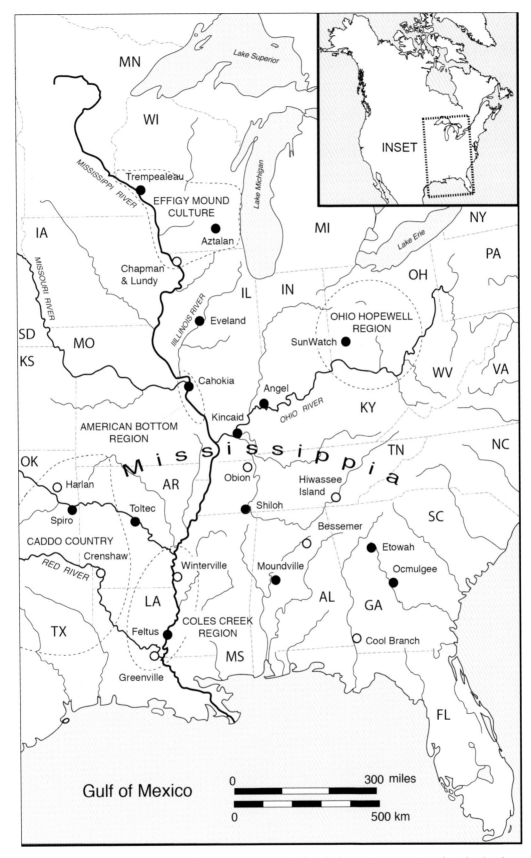

Map 3. Mississippian archaeological sites, regions, and related places. Sites mentioned in this book are shown as black circles.

Chronology of the Cahokian World

Date BCE ("before the common era")

3500   Earliest mound centers built in northern Louisiana and on the coastal plain of the Gulf of Mexico

1500   Great Late Archaic–period residential and pilgrimage complex built at Poverty Point; earliest pottery vessels in the eastern United States

500   The Woodland era begins, characterized by mixed foraging and horticultural lifestyles

100   Middle Woodland period begins, characterized by Hopewell mortuary ceremonialism, burial mounds, and great earthen embankments in the Ohio and Mississippi River valleys; earliest tobacco use and maize crops

Date CE ("of the common era")

400   Hopewell culture collapses; Late Woodland peoples become more insular, with less elaborate ceremonialism

600   Bow and arrow sweeps eastern North America; earliest chunkey gaming stones found in western Illinois and eastern Missouri

700–800   Earliest Coles Creek culture civic-ceremonial centers appear in lower Mississippi Valley, and Effigy Mound culture sites in the upper Mississippi Valley; maize cultivation intensifies along the Mississippi River from Little Rock, Arkansas, north to St. Louis, Missouri

900   Large Late Woodland village clusters develop along banks of Cahokia Creek on the Mississippi River floodplain opposite present-day St. Louis, Missouri; Caddoan culture appears in the trans-Mississippi South

1050 ± 20   Cahokia Creek village(s) replaced by the planned city of Cahokia; other subsidiary towns, ceremonial complexes, and many new farmsteads established near modern St. Louis during a short, large-scale construction phase

1050–1100   Toltec site in Arkansas depopulated; northern outposts founded; earliest Ohio River valley towns of Kincaid and Angel founded; Mound 72 sacrificial rites and large-scale religious festivals hosted at Cahokia

1100–1200   Other early Mississippian towns founded across the mid-South at places such as Shiloh, Tennessee; Mississippian migrations into southern Georgia

1200–1400   Oneota culture develops in upper Mississippi Valley; endemic organized violence across the eastern woodlands; Cahokia and adjacent regions are depopulated

1300–1500s   Tribal migrations south and west

1539–1543   Hernando de Soto's army penetrates deep into the southeastern North American interior; Francisco Vázquez de Coronado travels from the Southwest into Kansas attempting to find the legendary civilization of Quivira, described by a captured Pawnee guide

1540s–1600s   Continued European contacts; Old World diseases devastate American Indian populations

1699   French establish a colony on uninhabited land around ancient Cahokia

1810   Cahokia rediscovered by Henry Marie Brackenridge

1838   Last reported Morningstar sacrifice among the Skiri Pawnees

1850–1870s   Destruction of Cahokian pyramids in the St. Louis and East St. Louis precincts

1930s   Franklin D. Roosevelt's New Deal archaeology produces first comprehensive insights into Mississippian archaeology

1960s–2010s   Extensive excavations of Cahokian precincts under the auspices of the Illinois Department of Transportation and Illinois Historic Preservation Agency

Medieval Mississippians

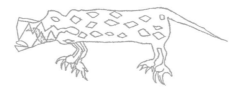

Figure 1.1. Artist's reconstruction of the central Cahokia precinct as viewed from the south.

Medieval Life in America's Heartland

Timothy R. Pauketat and Susan M. Alt

In the middle of the eleventh century, just as Europe entered its High Middle Ages, North American Indians in the Mississippi River valley began building their first true city, a place now called Cahokia (plate 1). Soon, new capital towns sprang up throughout what is now the US Southeast. Over each place towered from one to as many as two hundred flat-topped pyramids surmounted by large pole-and-thatch temples, residences, and warehouses of community priests and elites. Hereditary rulers or powerful councils led the citizens of individual provinces, who paid tribute and provisions to their leaders. Provinces rose to power or fell from it as their yearly corn crops and their alliances and wars with neighbors either succeeded or failed.

Archaeologists once called these people the Mound Builders, but today we know them simply as the Mississippians. In the early 1500s, Spanish explorers met their descendants in the Southeast— people living in towns, each still centered on one or more earthen pyramids topped with wooden temples and elite houses (chapter 12). In fields and farmsteads surrounding the towns, countryside dwellers grew maize (Indian corn), beans, and squash without the aid of draft animals. These people were all children of Cahokia, and the history of their civilization begins along the Mississippi River—that Great Father of Waters, that Nile of North America.

In about the year 1050 of the common era (CE, the equivalent of AD), the first Mississippians emerged seemingly full-blown among people still following earlier "Woodland" ways of life. Within just a few decades, Mississippians were colonizing new places and making their influence felt up and down the rivers of the continent's interior. Ultimately, they would alter the geopolitical landscape of North America, spread and intensify the cultivation of maize, and "Mississippianize" people from the Great Plains and Great Lakes to the Gulf coastal plain of today's Deep South. American history would have been different had the Mississippians never existed.

Much of the Mississippians' footprint on the landscape has been lost. In the nineteenth and early twentieth centuries, people who cared little about the history of American Indians flattened many of their great earthen monuments. Modern cities now sprawl over the ruins of ancient towns. But much still exists, both above ground and below, and researchers have been excavating and studying Mississippian archaeological sites for well over a century.

In the 1930s, the colossal excavations of southern archaeological sites carried out through President Franklin D. Roosevelt's New Deal blew open the doors to understanding the Mississippian past. Large crews of men and women excavated the remains of mounds, domestic houses, and cemeteries, beginning to detail the histories of Mississippian towns.

Figure 1.2. Central Cahokia, now crossed by a modern highway. Monks Mound (Mound 38) looms in the background, Mound 41 is the low rise in front of the trees, and Mound 42 is partly visible in the left foreground.

Archaeological research continues in the Midwest and Southeast today, complemented by the traditional histories and contemporary perspectives of Native people. In this book, archaeologists and other specialists, including two Native descendants of the Mississippians themselves, tell of the great ceremonial city of Cahokia, chart the florescence and eventual decline of the Mississippians, and offer snapshots of their way of life—their religion, architecture, farming economy, crafts, and much more.

People today seldom think of pre-Columbian American Indians as medieval, a word that usually denotes the European Middle Ages. But we like to call the Mississippians medieval because they were part of a worldwide phenomenon that climate scientists have labeled the Medieval Warm Period. During the three centuries from 950 to 1250 CE, the Earth's climate warmed by two or more degrees Fahrenheit. It seems a small change, but in many places it brought slightly heavier rainfall, enough that farmers were able to grow bigger, more reliable crops of grain. Herders found lusher grazing for their animals. Parts of the world where previously

no one had wanted to live started to look desirable.

As a result, the Medieval Warm Period saw cultures on the move and religions spreading across continents. In Europe during the tenth through the thirteenth centuries, devout Christians made arduous religious pilgrimages, launched bloody crusades, and built breathtaking cathedrals. In sub-Saharan Africa, trade cities emerged, founded on commerce with Arabs to the north and ocean-going Asians to the east. Having swept North Africa, Islam penetrated central Asia, where Genghis Khan was establishing his Mongol empire. Meanwhile, Hinduism spread eastward out of the cities of southern India into Cambodia, where it took form in the Khmer civilization's monumental stone temples, such as Angkor Wat.

In the Americas, too, the politics of the day carried religious overtones. New, independent cities arose in ancient Mexico following both the fall of the great imperial city of Teotihuacan in the 600s CE and the end of the Classic Maya kingdoms around 950. The people of these cities adopted distinctive Postclassic art styles and warrior symbolism

Figure 1.3. Excavations at the Grossmann site, which lay in a Mississippian farming area just southeast of Cahokia, carried out by a crew from the University of Illinois in 2001. Black plastic covers the remains of house basins and associated features.

and worshiped new gods, among them a serpentine wind god and a long-nosed, goggle-eyed rain deity. These gods and other Postclassic Mexican objects and ideas spread as far northwest as today's New Mexico and Arizona. The people of Chaco Canyon, New Mexico, for example, imported chocolate and colorful macaws from tropical Mexico, and until 1140 CE their great stone pueblos drew pilgrims from across the American Southwest.

We believe the eleventh-century emergence of Mississippian religion and lifeways was yet another manifestation of these Postclassic Mexican influences on the north, coupled with the climate trends seen all around the world during the Medieval Warm Period. In the American Midwest, an increase in average yearly precipitation accompanied the warmer weather, permitting maize farming to thrive. Without the food stores offered by maize and other domesticated plants, the populous, hierarchical, ever-spreading society of the Mississippians would never have gained a foothold.

Before about 200 BCE ("before the common era"), no one in eastern North America grew maize. During the early part of what archaeologists called the Woodland era, roughly 500 BCE to 1050 CE,

families in the eastern continent lived in hamlets and small villages of bent-pole wigwams, where they tended gardens of squash, sunflower, knotweed, lambsquarter, and maygrass—but no maize. They ate wild plants, too, and hunted game animals, fished, and collected mollusks.

This way of life began to change after 200 BCE, when some Woodland farmers experimented with growing small plots of maize and tobacco, two domesticated plants that had been carried north from Mexico. Corn caught on and became a staple in some places at some times—but not everywhere in eastern North America, and not always continuously.

For example, an early religious and cultural phenomenon along the Ohio and Mississippi Rivers, which researchers call the Hopewell tradition, was founded on a horticultural economy that sometimes included small plots of maize. But maize was not yet a staple crop and might have been reserved for use in special Hopewell ceremonies. From about 100 BCE to 400 CE, the leaders, priests, and shamans who conducted those ceremonies also designed imposing, geometrically shaped earthworks using sophisticated engineering and astronomical principles. After death, these men and women were entombed in great burial mounds. After the Hopewell religion and the regional confederacies dependent on it dissolved about 400 CE, maize farming and the ceremonies associated with it virtually disappeared for three hundred to four hundred years.

By the 800s, though, Late Woodland people living around present-day St. Louis, Missouri, among other places, had again begun growing maize in large quantities. One village there, the place soon to become the city of Cahokia, was prospering, with perhaps more than a thousand residents. Yet if anyone alive at the beginning of the Medieval Warm Period could have predicted that an American Indian city would arise in eastern North America, he or she would never have guessed it might happen where it did—in a quiet farming village in a swampy river bottom where no one had ever yet built a pyramid.

Mound building itself, as the Hopewell tradition shows, was hardly new in the Mississippi and Ohio River valleys. The roots of the tradition reached back as far as 3500 BCE, when some people living in what is now northeastern Louisiana began piling earth into eleven mounds as much as twenty-five feet high, all connected in an oval. Another well-known mound-building tradition, besides Hopewell, is the Effigy Mound culture. Prominent in the northern Mississippi Valley from 600 to 1050 CE, it tells us that maize farming was not necessary in order for people to build mounds. Effigy Mound people ate no corn but still buried their dead in small conical, linear, and animal-shaped mounds, all of which probably were effigies of mythical creatures or animal spirits and totems. These people, in modern-day Wisconsin, Iowa, Minnesota, and northern Illinois, would soon come face-to-face with Mississippians from downriver (chapter 8).

We think the actual founders of Cahokia were not Effigy Mound folk but a mix of local Late Woodland people who had long called the area home and immigrants from places to the south and southwest of the central Mississippi Valley. Along the southern river itself, in present-day Mississippi and Louisiana, lived people whom archaeologists know as the Coles Creek culture (chapter 2), probably speakers of a Siouan or Muskogean language.

West of the river, in southwestern Arkansas and eastern Oklahoma and Texas, lived speakers of languages in the Caddoan family. In between these two, in central Arkansas, resided people of an archaeological culture called Plum Bayou, whose ceremonial center, Toltec Mounds, was misnamed in the nineteenth century for the Toltec Indians of ancient Mexico.

Coles Creek people built flat-topped platform mounds that formed the centerpieces of large, impressive civic and ceremonial centers. Their four-sided pyramids fronted community plazas in ways reminiscent of Mexican cities far to the south, and the layout of their mound centers may have served as the prototype for Cahokia's city plan. Excavators have uncovered pieces of Coles Creek–style pottery at Cahokia and of Cahokia-made pottery at Coles Creek sites. Clearly, the two places had strong connections, and we see no reason why some Coles Creek people, even if just a few knowledgeable leaders, might not have carried their knowledge and wares directly to Cahokia at or just before its founding.

In the Arkansas and Red River valleys, the Woodland-era predecessors of the Caddoans—the "proto-Caddo" people—were already building small burial mounds by 900 CE. After 1050, they added Mississippian-style pyramidal mounds and plazas to their ceremonial centers and towns and became, in archaeologists' terminology, "Caddo-Mississippians." Just as Coles Creek artifacts strongly connect that culture with Cahokia, so prized Caddoan crafts discovered at Cahokia, such as exotic arrowheads and engraved marine shell cups, do likewise. And at the Caddo-Mississippian site of Spiro Mounds, high-status people were buried with many fine Cahokian things, among them carved red stone figurines (chapter 7). We think it likely that some of the residents of Cahokia, possibly including high-status dignitaries, hailed from Caddo country.

The Toltec site may be the most likely origin of high-status expatriates who migrated to Cahokia, because the date of Toltec's abandonment coincides closely with that of the great city's founding. After growing throughout the 900s CE, Toltec reached its peak in the early 1000s with eighteen mounds arranged in a distinctive pattern at an unusual angle (chapter 4), in a style much like that seen in the Coles Creek towns. Right around 1050, the inhabitants of Toltec left. Considering the similarities between the earthen monuments and architecture of Toltec and Cahokia, along with finds of Plum Bayou–style pottery at Cahokia, we believe some of the Toltec Mounds people migrated to Cahokia. Perhaps Plum Bayou folk from the great Toltec site, along with Coles Creek and proto-Caddo immigrants, were among the city's founding elites.

Exactly why such expatriates moved so far north of their homeland and precisely how their arrival altered the course of events at Cahokia are mysteries archaeologists are still trying to unravel. But together the newcomers and local Woodland villagers built a city, and spectacularly so—designing it, laying it out, artificially leveling the land, and raising its monuments using knowledge of engineering, geometry, and astronomy (chapters 3 and 4). This singular development nearly a thousand years ago transformed indigenous America so suddenly and so greatly that we call it Cahokia's Big Bang. The Cahokians innovated in architecture, introduced novel artifact styles, cleared vast tracts of land, and redesigned community life and agricultural production from the city center outward. Meanwhile, they fomented a new religion, which in a few years they would carry to far-off lands.

The Big Bang radiated outward almost immediately. Even as the pyramids of Cahokia began to rise, people in some way affiliated with the city—whether as colonists, allies, or even missionaries of a sort, converts to the new religion—traveled north up the Mississippi and founded villages and shrines in places now called the Eveland site, in Illinois, and the Aztalan and Trempealeau sites, in Wisconsin. In quick succession, "Cahokianized"

Figure 1.4. A Cahokian red stone smoking-pipe bowl found in Mound C at the Shiloh site, Tennessee.

locals, if not Cahokians themselves, established pyramid towns along rivers throughout the Midwest and Southeast, places now known as the archaeological sites of Angel, Kincaid, Shiloh, Moundville, and Ocmulgee, among others (map 3). To the south and southwest, the peoples who might have given birth to the Cahokians became increasingly Mississippianized in turn. Just as Caddoan speakers became Caddoan-Mississippians, so Coles Creek people became, in archaeologists' eyes, the "Plaquemine-Mississippian" people. By 1100, only fifty years after the founding of Cahokia, medieval

Figure 1.5. Reconstruction of a Mississippian-style pole-and-thatch house built with wall trenches. University of Illinois, 2001.

Mississippians occupied much of the American Midwest, Southeast, and trans-Mississippi South.

But what turned Woodland people into new Mississippians? What traits, beliefs, and objects did the Cahokians carry with them or export abroad? Most obviously, they brought to some places new, uniform town plans featuring earthen monuments and public plazas. They brought characteristic pottery and finely crafted ritual objects and ornaments, sometimes decorated with elaborate imagery. Some hallmarks of Mississipianism took everyday forms: the way people grew maize, built houses, wove fabric, made tools, crafted pots, and even played games (chapters 6, 9, 10, and 13). Archaeologists find, scattered far and wide in the ruins of Mississippian settlements and monumental centers, small artifacts that once signaled Mississippian beliefs and identity. Small red stone statuettes and smoking-pipe bowls, for example, carved in the shapes of goddesses, ancestors, culture heroes, spirit animals, and shamans, all intimate Cahokian connections. Made at Cahokia itself, these objects were either carried to new homes by Cahokian colonists or given to distant friends and allies as gifts.

One of the humblest but most universal traits of the Mississippian world—to archaeologists, an unfailing mark of people's genealogical connections to their Cahokian progenitors—was a technique of house construction unknown in the Mississippi Valley before 1050. From Trempealeau to the Chattahoochee, most Mississippians built their houses using *wall trenches*. Previously, Woodland people had dug individual holes for each wall post, a slow and tedious task performed by families and friends. At Cahokia around the time of the Big Bang, residents shifted almost overnight to digging shallow trenches using hoe blades. Work crews could then prefabricate walls on the ground before lifting them into the trench. As Cahokians and their allies extended their influence or control, they brought wall-trench construction to the hinterlands everywhere. Perhaps, by looking different from earlier houses, wall-trench buildings signaled an affiliation with the storied city of Cahokia, a set of new Mississippian ideals, and a powerful cultural or ethnic identity.

Underpinning everything else in the Mississippian way of life came a new religion. It almost certainly drew heavily on local, traditional religious practices, but it seems to have elevated key ancestral spirits, a distinctive goddess, and veneration of the moon, with which the goddess was probably affiliated (chapters 4 and 7).

Some features of the new religion probably originated as far away as Mexico, reaching the proto-Caddo and Coles Creek forebears of the Cahokians via the Gulf Coast of Mexico and Texas (map 2). Most North American archaeologists recognize that no sustained trade relations existed between Mexico and Cahokia or any of the other Mississippian civic-ceremonial centers. But over the centuries, travelers from the Midwest and trans-Mississippi South might well have ventured into Mexico, and vice versa, bringing home new ideas and religious practices.

One example of the new ideas is manifested in a swirly design called, when found at Cahokia, the "Ramey scroll" (plate 8). It is similar to motifs used in Mesoamerica that were often connected with a wind god or with conch shells from the Gulf of Mexico that were sometimes used as trumpets. Similarly, ornaments called "long-nosed god earpieces" (plate 4) might have manifested Mexican-inspired ideas. These ornaments depict goggled-eyed, long-nosed deities or spirits, much like images of the rain deity that Postclassic Mesoamericans began worshiping after the fall of Teotihuacan. Archaeologists think that elite Mississippian men wore them on their ears. Among the Ho-Chunk people of today's upper Midwest, stories of a culture hero, He Who Wears Human Heads As Earrings, persist. Legends tell that he has special powers. At one point he reincarnates his father's head, and at another, he marries a goddesslike woman. The idea of wearing gods on one's ears was practically unknown to the Woodland Indians before Cahokia but was widespread in Mesoamerica. Made at Cahokia rather than in

Wall Trench Architecture

Wall trenches served as the foundations for pole-supported walls in most Mississippian thatch-roofed wooden buildings. Minimally, wall trenches were narrow ditches, six to ten inches wide and one to two feet deep, around the perimeter of a building's floor. At Cahokia, builders prefabricated some walls, slipped them into their respective trenches, and tied them together at the corners around a floor set below ground surface. People wove pliable branches or strips of wood (wattle) between the wall posts and heaped earth against the outside to stabilize and weatherize the building. For house-size buildings and storage huts, bending the upper ends of the wall posts together produced bowed arbor roofs. For larger public buildings, the roof was a separate, gabled construction consisting of timbers and trusses supported by interior posts, all covered with thick bundles of dried grass or thatch.

In the Deep South, wall-trench houses resembled Cahokian ones but were less often set partly below ground. Rather than being buttressed by ramped earth, the walls of these buildings were daubed with mud mixed with grass. Some of the walls of the more important homes or public buildings were painted.

Figure 1.6. Wall trenches surrounding the floor of a building at the Grossmann site, Illinois.

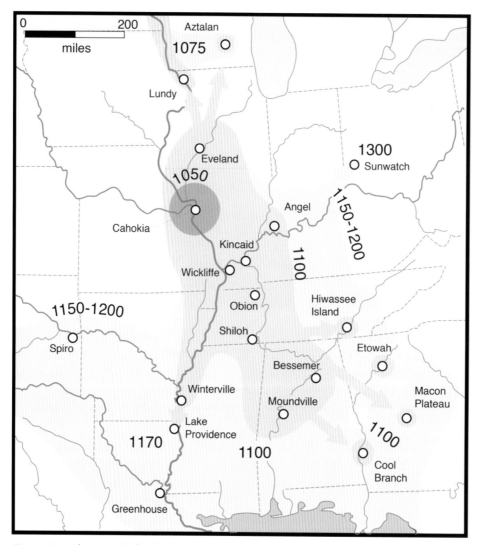

Figure 1.7. The spread of Cahokia-Mississippianism, based on the known distribution of wall-trench architecture.

Mexico, these prestigious ornaments have been uncovered in important burials and ritual deposits as far afield as Caddo country, the eastern Great Plains, and the Deep South.

Another idea that seems to connect Mexico and Cahokia, perhaps via the Caddo and Coles Creek peoples, was that of associating great upright poles with gods and ancestors. In central and western Mexico, posts and trees linked people on earth to various sky, wind, and rain gods. Still today, *voladores* along the Gulf Coast of Mexico perform ceremonies in which they "dance" in midair at the ends of ropes anchored to the tops of posts, all to appease the rain god. In late precolonial Mexico,

human sacrifice, too, was associated with wooden poles, the victims sometimes being tied to a pole or pole framework to enable the sky gods to receive the spirit offering. Aztec and Maya paintings, pottery decorations, and books of hieroglyphic writing (codices) also depict some gods in the form of a chipped-stone dagger that priests used to cut out the hearts of sacrificial victims. Interestingly, a locally made but Mexican-style chipped stone dagger, known as the "Ramey knife," appears in Cahokian deposits beginning at 1050 CE. Later forms of daggers and swords are known from other Mississippian centers, although their associations are often unclear.

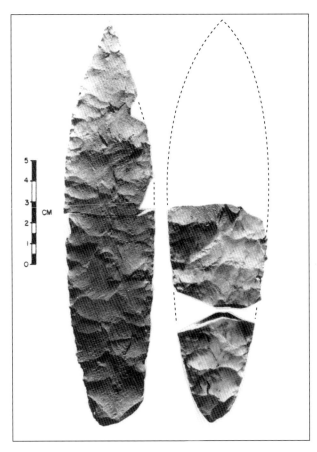

Figure 1.8. Cahokian daggers, or "Ramey knives," from a small site south of Cahokia.

Coles Creek people had been planting vertical posts on the tops of mounds since at least 400 CE. Cahokians continued the practice, but they placed posts in many locations, sometimes in rows aligned with distant landmarks and celestial events. At Cahokia and other Mississippian mound sites, posts were monumentally large: three feet in diameter and sixty feet high. Sometimes Mississippians painted and possibly carved their posts. Never did they leave them to rot in place; instead, they cared for them and ceremonially moved them from time to time. At Cahokia, pulling the great post from the ground was sometimes an occasion for human sacrifice.

Almost every human society in history has seen a time when it deemed human sacrifice necessary to satisfy the gods or some other forces governing existence, who could restore order and abundance when famine or political upheaval struck. In midwestern and southeastern North America, human sacrifice was virtually unknown as a public specta-

cle before Cahokia, although several likely sacrificed women and possibly children are known from one mound in the Coles Creek region dating to about 800 CE. Cahokians, however, occasionally sacrificed from one to as many as fifty-three persons, usually women (chapter 3). A single body might be buried in a pit where a symbolic upright post had stood, after the post was ritually removed. Even more dramatically, whole groups of victims might be buried together above a former post pit or under an earthen mound.

This kind and scale of human sacrifice is not yet known to have existed at other Mississippian towns. Nevertheless, great Mississippian places such as Shiloh, Ocmulgee, Etowah, and Moundville were sacred centers of worship as well as seats of government. Much of their power and influence rested on religion. That people might experience all the powers of distant lands and the cosmos at such places could even have been the reason Cahokia—a novel political capital and densely populated city—succeeded in the first place. It might explain the rapid founding of outposts and copycat towns, and it might account for the rapid and widespread adoption of all things Mississippian, from wall-trench houses to gods worn on the ears. In other words, a deep-seated desire to be in tune with the universe and its great unseen powers could be a reason people joined Mississippian civilization.

At Cahokia and across the Mississippian world, religion was probably inseparable from government, society, and economy. Leaders, priests, and shamans, we think, created rules, organized their followers' lives, and traveled great distances to obtain materials needed to keep the world in balance. They performed religious rituals including great processions, dances in the public plazas, and a hugely popular sport, a game now called chunkey. They presided over ceremonial feasts in which participants consumed the best fruits, berries, meats, soups, and drinks—among the last, a caffeinated tea, the "black drink," made from leaves of an exotic holly bush and drunk from special mugs (plates 2 and 5).

As in Europe during the Middle Ages, so in midwestern and southeastern North America religion was the force that unified people. In this way, the Mississippians were as medieval as any other civilization of their time. Few empires held sway over the rest of the medieval world, and we are fairly certain that there was no sustained Mississippian empire, either. Intruding Mississippians might have made enemies of local people, but no Mississippian army routinely marched the length and breath of the Mississippi valley, and Cahokia was no imperial city, at least not for long. Rather, the Mississippian world grew to look more like medieval Japan, where feudal, warrior societies and religion defined social life and cultural history.

For Cahokia and the early Mississippians, this unifying religious force assumed a life of its own. Some outposts, shrines, and sister complexes attest to Cahokians proselytizing outsiders, and pilgrims journeyed to Cahokia to take part in the great events and lucrative trade that animated the cosmopolitan city (chapters 11 and 15; plate 3). People as far away as present-day Georgia looked to the fabled mound city on the Mississippi for inspiration (chapter 17).

Of course in all societies, medieval or otherwise, political unifications and territorial conquests can be fleeting. As it happened, by 1350 all the residents of Cahokia had departed, dispersing in every direction. Political or military mishaps, an uptick in organized violence, a loss of faith, and crop failures might all have been to blame—possibly in that order. After 1200, nearly all significant Mississippian population centers were fortified; apparently, some of Cahokia's former colonies and friends became its foes. Sometimes these places were sacked and burned. Cahokians might well have been the aggressors along the central Mississippi Valley and up into the Illinois River valley (chapter 14). Meanwhile, the Medieval Warm Period was drawing to a close. Temperatures were cooling, and less rain fell on farmers' crops.

The new political landscape of the times may be depicted in a rare rock-art map that sits on the edge of the Mississippi River at a place called Thebes Gap. There, some ancient cartographer pecked into the rock a long squiggly line, likely depicting the Mississippi River, together with other lines, dots, a bird, an eye, and a moccasin print. Perhaps these motifs indicate trails, places, and the identities of

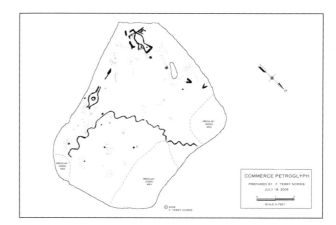

Figure 1.9. Rock-art map of the Mississippi. *Top*: a drawing of the map; *bottom*: the rock's position on the bank of the Mississippi River.

people affiliated with towns in the region, all of which date later than 1200.

By 1400, most central Mississippi Valley towns had emptied. To the north and northwest, violence was out of control among Mississippianized tribes whom archaeologists call the Oneota (chapter 5). Mississippian peoples in the Deep South had become balkanized into warring provinces. These were the peoples who met the Europeans after 1492 and who were soon devastated by European diseases, the Caribbean slave trade, and ever-escalating warfare between Native tribes and European powers. The medieval Mississippian world had ended.

Yet the descendants of Cahokians and other Mississippians endure, and the remains of their ancient city, capital towns, and ceremonial centers have much to teach us about how civilizations happened in the past and how all Americans today are connected to that past. Cahokia and its followers and allies were responsible for the culinary practices, religious beliefs, cultural rules, social institutions, and tribal affiliations of many indigenous midwestern and southern peoples. It was they who fed and sheltered European explorers, warred with the United States, and defined the early American experience, helping to make us all what we are today.

Timothy R. Pauketat is a professor of anthropology and medieval studies at the University of Illinois who is interested in the broad relationships between ancient cosmologies, cities, and the everyday experiences of agricultural peoples. He has directed excavations from Cahokia north to Trempealeau, and his recent books include *An Archaeology of the Cosmos* (2013) and *Cahokia: Ancient North America's Great City on the Mississippi* (2009).

Susan M. Alt is an associate professor of anthropology at Indiana University, Bloomington, with interests in Mississippian origins, migrations, violence, gender, and the built environment. Her current research concerns relationships between Cahokia, the Emerald complex, and the Yankeetown culture of southwestern Indiana. She is the editor of *Ancient Complexities: New Perspectives in Pre-Columbian North America* (2010).

Figure 2.1. The Feltus site as painted in 1850 by John Egan from an 1846 field drawing by William T. W. Dickeson, the younger brother of Montroville W. Dickeson. The four main mounds are in their correct positions, but the artist added extra mounds on the left and right and made the summits rounded rather than flat. The two circular basins in front of the mounds were probably created by erosion.

Cahokia's Coles Creek Predecessors

Vincas P. Steponaitis, Megan C. Kassabaum, and John W. O'Hear

Some of the founding ideas undergirding Cahokia came from a mound-building culture that flourished between 700 and 1200 CE in the southern Mississippi Valley, in the present-day states of Mississippi and Louisiana. Archaeologists recognize the people who lived there as members of the Coles Creek culture, who were themselves heirs to a tradition of mound building stretching back as far as 3500 BCE. Unlike the far more populous Cahokians, who relied on large stores of maize to fuel workers and feed gathered throngs of worshippers, the Coles Creek people, up until the twelfth century, accomplished what they did without growing corn. The natural bounty of the river and its floodplains made the Coles Creek homeland a hunter, fisher, and forager's paradise where people could live well and build mounds too, all by hunting, collecting wild foods, and gardening native plants.

Coles Creek people built civic-ceremonial centers dominated by flat-topped, rectangular mounds surrounding open plazas—a site plan that became the prototype for Cahokia and later Mississippian centers. Archaeologists call these sorts of earthworks *platform mounds* or *truncated pyramids*, because their tops were leveled flat, unlike the rounded tops of other mounds.

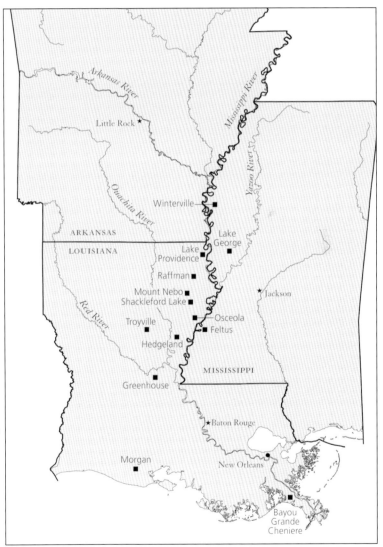

Figure 2.2. The lower Mississippi River valley, showing locations of excavated Coles Creek mound centers.

The Caddo Conundrum

Timothy R. Pauketat

Figure 2.3. A Cahokia-made "Spiro Engraved" beaker, two and a half inches tall and wide, found at Cahokia.

The Mississippi, Red, and Arkansas Rivers drain the hardwood and pine forests of the coastal plain west of the Mississippi River. This region is sometimes called the trans-Mississippi South, and historically it was the homeland of people who spoke distinctive Caddoan language dialects. Their history was in some ways connected to that of the Coles Creek and Cahokian peoples. All were "Mississippianized" during the Medieval Warm Period. In the case of the Caddos, archaeologists remain uncertain: were they on the receiving end of ideas emanating out of Cahokia, or did proto-Caddos in the 900s or 1000s help bring about the rise of Cahokia?

For years archaeologists have dug up pieces of beakers and bowls at Cahokia that were decorated with elaborate decorations reminiscent of Coles Creek and Caddo cultures, some dating to just before and others after Cahokia's Big Bang moment around the year 1050. Most were made at Cahokia and, judging from chemical tests, Cahokians likely used them to serve yaupon-holly tea, or "black drink," the leaves for which were native to the trans-Mississippi South. These beakers and bowls suggest an early connection between Cahokian, Coles Creek, and proto-Caddoan peoples; perhaps some of the Cahokian dishes were even made by immigrant Caddo and Coles Creek potters.

Historical connections of some kind existed between Cahokians and the Caddos at key sites such as Spiro Mounds, in eastern Oklahoma. The high-status dead of Spiro were buried with Cahokian objects, among them carved red stone, or "flint clay," figurines (chapter 7). Apparently, the Spiroans prized their Cahokian connections or heritage. Cahokians, in turn, possessed a few of the famous engraved marine shell cups that were buried in great numbers at Spiro. No one has yet proved where these Gulf Coast shells were engraved or who the engravers were, although the art style appears derived from Cahokia.

What is certain is that the ancient Caddos were the ancestors of the historic Caddo tribe, whose descendants today are citizens of the Caddo Nation in Oklahoma. Perhaps through mutual influence between Spiro and Cahokia, Mississippian culture helped define what we know today as Caddo culture, or vice versa. Certainly, the appearance of the Caddos as a distinctive linguistic and ethnic group dates to the time when Cahokia was on the rise.

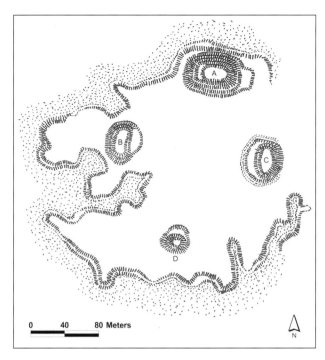

Figure 2.4. The Feltus site. Mound D was destroyed around 1940; its size and location have been reconstructed from an 1852 survey and old aerial photographs. The mounds sit on an isolated landform flanked by steep slopes on three sides.

Native peoples of the Deep South had been building platform mounds since the first century BCE, but initially these were rare in comparison with rounded ones. Early platform mounds seldom had buildings on top; rather, their summits show evidence of free-standing posts, burned areas, and refuse deposits containing broken pottery and food remains. Archaeologist Vernon Knight has argued convincingly that such mounds served as public stages for periodic world-renewal ceremonies, which involved feasting and the setting in and later pulling up of wooden posts. Usually small, the early platform mounds saw only one or two stages of construction apiece before being decommissioned with a covering of earth.

From these antecedents, a new architectural pattern crystallized in the lower Mississippi Valley by 800 CE—the Coles Creek pattern, in which ceremonial centers typically consisted of two to four platform mounds arranged around an open plaza. The mounds often (but not always) supported wooden buildings, though we do not know yet what these earliest buildings were used for. The newer platform mounds tended to be larger than their predecessors and show more stages of construction, suggesting greater continuity of use. People of the early Caddo culture and their Plum Bayou culture neighbors, who lived along the Arkansas and Red Rivers to the west, adopted this pattern, too. Flat-topped monuments became ubiquitous in the lower Mississippi Valley even as post-related rituals and feasting continued. Together, these monuments and rituals became a major piece of the historical substrate from which the mound and post rituals of the medieval Mississippians emerged.

The layouts of Coles Creek–type mound centers look similar enough that researchers believe they conformed to a broadly shared, relatively formal plan. Maybe the sites served as the central places of large political territories. Few people, if any, actually lived in the mound centers—perhaps only community and religious leaders and their families. Most ordinary people lived in scattered outlying settlements and gathered at the mounds periodically for ceremonies and feasts.

Archaeologists have excavated relatively few Coles Creek centers, and only a handful thoroughly enough to gain a good understanding of the construction and uses of the mounds. One site, however—the Feltus Mounds in southwestern Mississippi—has a history of archaeological investigations going back to the 1840s, when a Philadelphia physician named Montroville W. Dickeson collected artifacts and dug into one of the mounds. In 1852, Mississippi's first state geologist, Benjamin L. C. Wailes, made a map of the site. Archaeologist Warren King Moorehead excavated into two of the mounds in 1924, and years later, in 1971, a crew with Harvard University's Lower Mississippi Survey carried out a small dig. Since 2006, we have collaborated in four seasons of excavation at Feltus. Most of our data are still being analyzed, but our preliminary findings, together with the results of earlier investigations, paint an interesting picture of the site's history and the kinds of public rituals that took place there—rituals that no doubt foreshadowed even grander ones to come at Cahokia.

Feltus mounds sit on a hundred-foot-high bluff

Figure 2.5. Coles Creek pottery vessels. The designs were typically incised or stamped into the vessel's surface while the clay was still wet.

overlooking the Mississippi River floodplain. Of its four original mounds, three survive today. The site's builders placed the mounds at the cardinal points around a plaza: Mound A to the north, Mound B to the west, Mound C to the east, and Mound D, now destroyed, to the south. The three surviving mounds have flat summits, but judging from a sketch made by Benjamin Wailes in the 1850s, Mound D was dome shaped. A moat encircled at least Mound C. Radiocarbon dates reveal that people used the site for three and a half centuries, from approximately 750 to 1100 CE—that is, from well before the Mississippian period into its early decades.

The earliest residents of Feltus erected no mounds but did leave a large oval pile of refuse—pottery, animal bones, and plant remains—around the edges of the plaza. We think this trash pile, or midden, held the remains of ceremonial feasts associated with symbolic wooden posts placed upright on the southern side of the oval. The free-standing

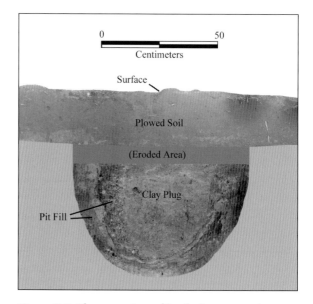

Figure 2.6. Photomosaic profile of a large post pit near Mound D, Feltus. Below about nine inches of plowed soil lay a central clay plug where the post once stood and, around that, dirt rich in charcoal and ash. The eroded area was washed away by heavy rain before a photograph could be taken.

Figure 2.7. Mound A at the Feltus site, as photographed by Warren King Moorehead in 1924.

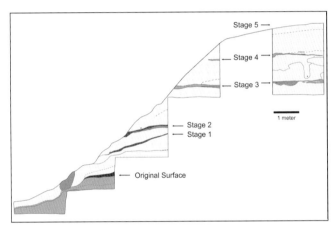

Figure 2.8. Profile of a trench dug into the west flank of Mound B, showing five stages of construction. The summits of the first two stages were marked by clay veneers. The summits of the third and fourth stages were burned and contained post holes, presumably from wooden buildings. Any prepared floors or features that once existed on the final summit (Stage 5) have been obliterated by erosion.

posts ranged from six inches to more than a foot in diameter and were set in pits up to three feet deep. Around the posts, someone packed the holes with earth containing ash and charcoal, probably from hearths or cooking pits, as well as objects such as tobacco pipes, bear bones, and, in one case, jumbled bones of human infants. After residents later

pulled the posts out, they refilled the holes, usually with clean brown clay. In one area about fifteen feet across, we found a cluster of more than twenty pits where posts had been planted and removed repeatedly, sometimes on the same spot. One pit yielded a radiocarbon date of 780 CE, give or take fifty years.

About thirty feet east of these posts lay a cluster of large pits filled with broken pottery, animal bones, and other trash. Many of the pottery vessels were unusually large, and radiocarbon dates showed that the pits and the nearby posts were contemporary with each other. That is why we think the trash came from public feasting connected with ceremonies involving the wooden posts. Indeed, we suspect that most of the refuse around the early Feltus plaza was discarded during such feasts.

In the 900s, construction began on Mounds A and B and, we presume, on C and D. Each mound went up in stages. First, workers piled up earth to a certain height, packing it hard and leveling the top. People then used the summit for a while but eventually dismantled any wooden structures they had raised there. Workers now added a new layer of construction fill, making the mound taller and beginning the cycle again. As a result, each mound is something like a layer cake, with as many as five construction episodes.

Since 2006 we have excavated trenches into a flank of each standing mound. Our excavations, together with Moorehead's work in 1924, show that the Feltus people used each mound in a different way.

They built Mound A in three stages, until it reached a height of twenty-three feet. Before starting construction, people evidently held a public ceremony in which they planted and then pulled ceremonial posts and feasted, leaving the post pits and trash from the meal on the spot where the mound was about to be built. Yet surprisingly, the mound's successive summits showed a very different pattern of use. All these surfaces were clean; we have yet to find any substantial midden or evidence of buildings. The only signs of use on the summits were scattered charcoal from burning and large, bathtub-shaped fire pits, which people probably used for cooking large animals, like modern barbeque pits.

Mound B, some twenty feet high, went up in five stages. Unlike at Mound A, we found no signs of feasting at its base, and each of its summits was faced with a thin veneer of yellow or black soil. On the third and fourth summits we uncovered post holes and large, fire-reddened areas—good indications that these surfaces once supported wooden buildings or other structures that were burned as part of "decommissioning" before a new stage went up. In one of Mound B's stages, users threw refuse off the edge of the summit, leaving a thick midden down the mound's flank. We have not yet finished studying the trash in this midden, so we do not know yet just what people were doing on Mound B.

Mounds C and D, the two smallest mounds at ten to thirteen feet high, served as burial places. When Moorehead excavated them in 1924, each contained many bundles of disarticulated human bones—the typical pattern at Coles Creek sites, where funerals were communal events. Bones and bodies in various stages of decay, which had been temporarily kept in mortuary temples, were reburied together in mass graves, simply and without grave goods. Interestingly, in Mound C all the bones lay within two feet of the mound's last summit, meaning that they were placed there late in the mound's history. Perhaps the mass burial was part of a decommissioning ceremony for an associated mortuary temple or for the mound itself. The moat surrounding Mound C might have been what archaeologist Robert Hall, referring to similar moats throughout the ancient South and Midwest, called a "spirit barrier," meant to keep the spirits of the dead out of the world of the living.

Each of the four mounds on the site, then, had a distinctive history and purpose. Mound A had a clean summit with cooking pits and no buildings; Mound B had burned floors with wooden structures and flank middens; and Mounds C and D served as mortuaries, at least late in their histories. We believe these differences reflect the role each mound played in public ceremonies at Feltus—ceremonies in which people repeatedly set and removed large wooden posts, feasted, and built earthen mounds.

Differences in mound use like this were not unique to Feltus. Archaeologists have observed them at other contemporary sites in southern Mississippi, Arkansas, and northern Louisiana. For example, the largest mound at the Raffman site had no obvious middens or buildings on its successive summits, just like our Mound A. At the Greenhouse site, excavated in the 1930s, one mound had burned summits and another did not; this site also had dozens of bathtub-shaped fire pits. And on the original ground surface beneath the "Great Mound" at Troyville—a mound destroyed for bridge construction in 1931—people had laid down rows of large wooden posts and then buried them under the mound. It is not hard to imagine Troyville residents using the posts in rituals like the ones at Feltus.

Setting large posts and staging public feasts were not activities unique to the lower Mississippi Valley in pre-Mississippian times. People across eastern North America had been holding such ceremonies for at least two thousand years. But the Mississippians were about to take both public rituals and the mound-and-plaza layout to new scales of size and spectacle, starting at Cahokia around 1050 CE and eventually spreading over much of the South and Midwest. Just as people from the Coles Creek area must have helped shape Cahokia at its founding, so Cahokians returned the favor, contacting and sharing ideas with their Coles Creek cousins some four hundred miles to the south. By the 1100s, people from the two regions regularly exchanged pottery and participated in each other's ceremonies. We could ask for no better example of how interconnected the people of the medieval Mississippian world came to be.

Vincas P. Steponaitis is a professor of anthropology, director of the Research Laboratories of Archaeology, and chair of the Curriculum in Archaeology at the University of North Carolina at Chapel Hill. He studies the precolonial Indian cultures of the American South, focusing especially on their art styles, settlements, and political organization. Since 2006 he has co-directed excavations at Feltus.

Megan C. Kassabaum completed her dissertation at the University of North Carolina at Chapel Hill in 2014. She used ceramic, floral, and faunal data to study the activities that took place at Feltus, especially communal ritual activities. She is now assistant professor in the Department of Anthropology and Weingarten Assistant Curator for North America at the Museum of Anthropology and Archaeology at the University of Pennsylvania, where she continues her work on Coles Creek sites in the lower Mississippi Valley.

John W. O'Hear is the principal of J. W. O'Hear Consulting, an adjunct senior research associate in the Department of Sociology and Anthropology at the University of Mississippi, and, since 2006, co-director of excavations at Feltus.

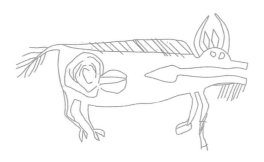

Figure 3.1. The head of a Cahokian goddess statuette carved from red stone.

An American Indian City

three

Timothy R. Pauketat, Thomas E. Emerson, Michael G. Farkas, and Sarah E. Baires

More than four centuries after being abandoned, the ancient American Indian city of Cahokia lay in ruins. It had once covered seven or eight square miles, its "capital zone" spanning three major precincts. Now, in 1810, the nearly two hundred packed-earth pyramids of the sprawling complex were merely weed-covered mounds of earth. All traces of the imposing wooden structures that once topped the flat summits of these earthen monu-

ments had long since decayed to dust. Around the mounds, fields sprinkled with potsherds, bones, and bits of flint only hinted at busy neighborhoods where families lived in modest pole-and-thatch houses.

Yet even in 1810, one astonished visitor sensed the former stateliness of the ruined city. Henry Marie Brackenridge, a young frontier lawyer, wrote in his journal that the place's pyramids were spaced

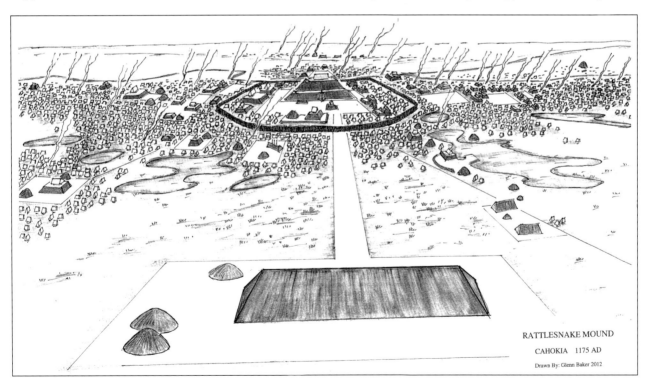

RATTLESNAKE MOUND
CAHOKIA   1175 AD
Drawn By: Glenn Baker 2012

Figure 3.2. Artist's view of the central precinct of Cahokia at about 1175 CE, looking north from Rattlesnake Mound.

Figure 3.3. Destruction of Powell Mound, near the western edge of central Cahokia. The landowner removed the mound in 1930 to increase his farm's tillable acreage.

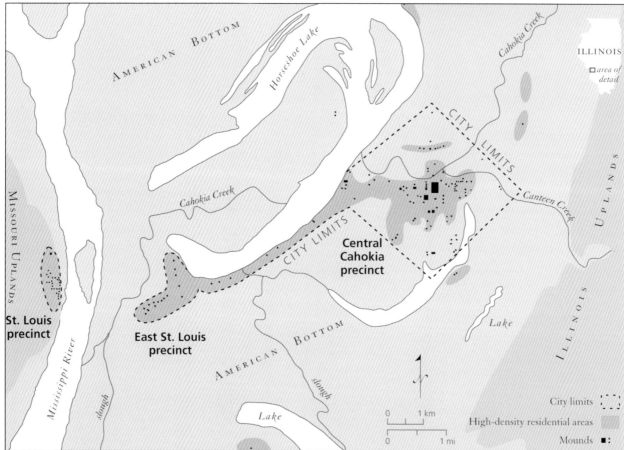

Figure 3.4. The three precincts of Cahokia: central, or "downtown," Cahokia, St. Louis, and East St. Louis.

"at regular distances from each other" and "appeared to observe some order." Surely, he concluded, "a very populous town had once existed here, similar to those of Mexico, described by the first conquerors."

Today, visitors can see some of the eroded pyramids of this ancient city, but its temples, its spacious plazas, and the houses of its ordinary residents have all returned to the earth. For more than two centuries, American farmers have plowed and planted the topsoil over Cahokia. By 1900, industrious Americans had destroyed the seventy to eighty pyramids of two of the city's former precincts, one now in modern St. Louis, Missouri, and the other beneath present-day East St. Louis.

Railroad engineers in the late 1800s planned to

Figure 3.5. Artist's view of the East St. Louis precinct of Cahokia at about 1150 CE.

Figure 3.6. Excavation of the base of a massive cypress post at the Mitchell site, part of greater Cahokia. Posts at Cahokia, East St. Louis, and St. Louis had diameters similar to this three-foot-wide section. When upright, they projected about thirty feet into the air.

remove even the largest pyramids of the central Cahokia precinct, which archaeologists sometimes call "downtown Cahokia." Fortunately for later researchers and the public, they were unable to purchase the biggest mounds from their private landowners, and the plan flopped. But twentieth-century developers of factories, warehouses, and

neighborhoods destroyed more of the archaeological landscape, often by bulldozing entire landforms and erasing archaeological sites. We estimate that more than half of greater Cahokia's archaeological deposits —those lying within the one thousand to two thousand square miles of southwestern Illinois and eastern Missouri centered on the capital zone— have been thoroughly disturbed if not completely destroyed.

Cahokia, though, was the behemoth of ancient American history, so large that portions of it survived against seemingly impossible odds. In surface area and population, Cahokia's three precincts together were larger than St. Louis was before 1840. They rivaled some of the early cities of Mesopotamia, China, Mexico, and Peru. No other native settlement of any sort in eastern North America ever attained such a size. A few other Mississippian towns, a few large Plains Indian villages, and an Iroquois village or two reached populations of two thousand souls; Cahokia was at least five times bigger.

Thanks to the city's massiveness, more than a square mile of the now-moundless East St. Louis precinct still sits intact under modern streets and buildings. In excavated parcels, we have discovered that the ancient precinct's walled compounds and

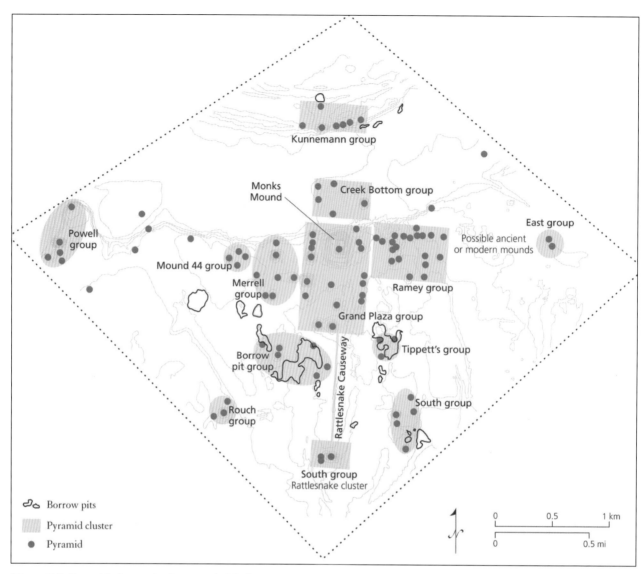

Figure 3.7. Pyramid clusters in the central Cahokia precinct.

unwalled neighborhoods were rigidly aligned to an off-cardinal grid oriented ten degrees west of north. Monumental posts measuring up to three feet in diameter and standing as much as thirty feet high, sometimes placed in rows, marked the precinct's organizational axes. Presumably, such posts were also symbolic connections between the sky, the spirits of the ancestors, and the people of Cahokia. Specific posts might have represented individual ancestors or at least the pyramids, precincts, or neighborhoods with which the ancestors were associated.

This urban design and its monuments complement those known from downtown Cahokia, some twenty-two hundred acres of which have been preserved as an Illinois state historic site since 1925. With some difficulty, we can today recognize three monumental vertebrae in the original spine of downtown Cahokia—a great central pyramid, known as Monks Mound, an adjacent Grand Plaza, and an arrow-straight southern causeway (plate 7). All three are rigidly aligned to this precinct's off-cardinal axis, which, unlike the axis of the East St. Louis precinct, is oriented five degrees east of north.

Looming one hundred feet over the surrounding precinct, the principal pyramid, Monks Mound, went up in a few short construction episodes between 1050 and 1150 CE. From the summit of its three (possibly four) stacked terraces, Cahokian leaders, priests, and other dignitaries might have watched, and been watched by, the people. A small conical mound, likely a marker of the very center of Cahokia—the axis mundi, the place where the horizontal realm of earth meets heaven above—sat on the right front of the pyramid's flat second terrace. Behind it stood several elaborate pole-and-thatch buildings, including a hall or temple as large as some medieval European palaces. The great building was the largest known at Cahokia, covering at least forty-three hundred square feet and perhaps many more, depending on whether or not an outer wall was a palisade. Its wall posts had been planed with adzes to square them off.

Next to this building, an upright post rose nearly twenty feet skyward. It might have been an important marker of a powerful ancestral spirit. Nelson Reed, the archaeologist who excavated it, thought it might also have been a lightning rod. Copper bits found where the post wood had once been could mean that part of it was sheathed in copper. When the excavators put up a modern post in the same spot, lightning struck it repeatedly. Imagine the effects of such lightning strikes in the past on people who witnessed them from below.

Laid out at the foot of Monks Mound was the Grand Plaza, a great, artificially leveled community square. Covering nearly fifty acres, this spacious plaza could easily have held the entire population of the city during special celebrations. It doubtless formed the hub of social and ceremonial life in downtown Cahokia. In an enormous pit adjacent to the plaza—a trench three hundred feet long, sixty feet wide, and nine feet deep—excavators have found debris from religious festivals held on the plaza. Cahokian workers dug the pit shortly after 1050 to obtain earth to build up the plaza and pyramids. Afterward, people filled it with a rich assortment of refuse from the ritual events of the early years: uneaten food, broken pots, tobacco seeds, chips of wood made when posts were debarked and planed, burned temple roofs, parts of cedar brooms, and the ashes of celebratory fires.

Additional borrow pits like this, dug by Cahokians to obtain earth for their many construc-

tion projects, dot the swampy, low-lying southern end of the downtown precinct. For certain mounds, builders preferred this area's heavy, black, water-logged clays. The sticky mud might also have been meaningful symbolically. In the historic period, creation stories of indigenous peoples living along the central Mississippi Valley often told of an "earth diver," a mythical spider or other animal who, at the dawn of time, created the world by piling up mud retrieved from the bottom of primordial waters. Building a mound with mud from the swamp bottom might have been a physical, full-bodied reenactment of the story of creation.

Clearly, the watery, muddy, southern realm of Cahokia was important in the eyes of city leaders. There they oversaw the building of what probably were two offertory platforms projecting out into clay-mining pits, as well as several burial mounds of a type called "ridge-top" mounds. Rather than having flat tops, these rectangular mounds had peaked summits, like the roof of a house, with a central ridgeline.

Most spectacularly, the early Cahokians built through the swamp a half-mile-long elevated causeway leading from Monks Mound south to one of the ridge-top burial mounds, Mound 66. In 1929, archaeologist Warren Moorehead nicknamed that tumulus "Rattlesnake Mound," so we now call the earthen road "Rattlesnake Causeway." Moorehead described the road as "an elevation flanked by two ponds or depressions. Old observers used to call this a causeway leading to other mounds." At about eighty feet wide and up to two feet thick, the causeway can be seen in LiDAR and other satellite imagery. Today, a modern railroad crosses the causeway north of Rattlesnake Mound, and in the early 1900s, railroad workers scooped dirt from the edge of the ancient avenue to build the berm for a railroad spur running along the top of the causeway. The spur, too, although it was left unfinished, can be seen in LiDAR images (plate 10).

Because Rattlesnake Causeway runs at a compass bearing five degrees off a true north-south line—just as the primary mounds and plaza of downtown Cahokia do—the road might have served as the actual baseline for the central precinct's plan. Archaeoastronomer William Romain

LiDAR

A technology called LiDAR, which stands for Light Detection and Ranging, has proved a boon to archaeologists in recent years. Through LiDAR, scientists map the surface of the earth using laser scanners mounted on aircraft. The scanner shoots many laser beams at once, and a certain percentage of them penetrate vegetation such as forest canopy, allowing an unobstructed view of the earth's surface. The amount of time between each laser pulse and its reflection from the surface below is measured to calculate the target's precise elevation and location. Using many measurements, researchers produce contour maps of great accuracy. LiDAR images readily show the shapes and outlines of ancient mounds and allow subtle features such as causeways and depressions be detected for perhaps the first time in centuries.

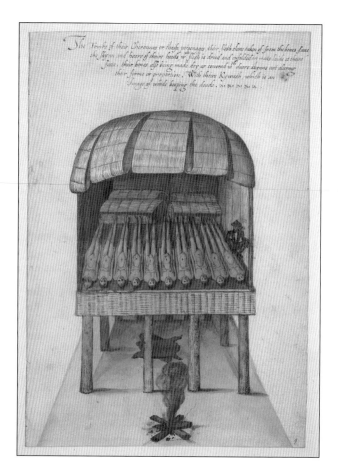

Figure 3.8. A 1564 painting by Jacques Le Moyne, showing a mortuary temple, or charnel house, containing the bodies of "chief personages" of Algonkian people in colonial Carolina. At the feet of the deceased lie baskets of ancestral bones; to the right, a carved wooden image watches over the dead.

(chapter 4) believes this baseline was the vertical axis of a large design square based on the point at which the full moon rose at its southern extreme above the bluffs to the east, an event that happened once every 18.6 years. Cahokians no doubt watched the rising sun on the horizon throughout the year, too, but Romain's hypothesis pins the overall order of the city to an astronomical observation of the moon.

Sarah Baires, who recently excavated parts of the causeway, believes it might have linked the Cahokians metaphorically to the realm of the dead. A walk along this causeway from the Grand Plaza to Rattlesnake Mound might have been a spiritual journey from the world of the living to the place of the dead, much in the way souls, according to a common American Indian belief, traveled along the Milky Way, the great "Path of Souls" in the night sky. Around the ridge-top mounds, and likely along the causeway as well, stood charnel buildings that held bodies of the deceased, scaffolds on which corpses were exposed to the elements, and ancestral temples where priests carefully curated the

defleshed bones of the long dead. Some of the bones buried in the mounds came from people whose lives had been sacrificed during ceremonies conducted every few years.

Cahokia was a place of such scale that it humbled the visitor. Like the Grand Plaza and its adjacent pyramids, secondary plazas and other mounds seem to have been arranged together in great blocks of space. William Romain believes such blocks to have been the original design features of the city. Site archaeologist Melvin Fowler, who identified at least a dozen of these lesser mound-and-plaza groups in the 1970s, believed some of them were the centers of residential neighborhoods or subcommunities. Some perhaps were home to weavers, flint knappers, copper workers, potters, or other craftspeople who made stone ax heads or shell beads,

Human Sacrifice at Cahokia

Susan M. Alt

In the summer of 2012, two students working on our dig at the Emerald site in Lebanon, Illinois, were carefully excavating what would turn out to be a six-foot-deep pit that once held an upright post some two feet in diameter. Because of the great heights of such posts, native excavators dug their pits with long ramps slanting down to where the base of the post would rest. The students were following the ramp to its bottom, and about halfway down, they scraped into bone. All work on the feature stopped, and we made new plans to determine whether the bone was human. If so, Illinois state law required that we stop all excavation of the feature and rebury the remains.

We already knew that the bodies of young women had been found in other post pits around Cahokia, their lives apparently having been sacrificed as offerings to important places. The spots where the posts stood were likely sacred, and some archaeologists believe the poles themselves were like people, having spirits and needing to be cared for or prayed to.

So far, all the bodies identified in post pits at greater Cahokia have been female. One of two women in post pits in the East St. Louis precinct apparently had her legs and wrists tied when she was placed in the pit. Twenty-two women buried over a former post pit beneath Cahokia's Mound 72 are also suspected to have been sacrifices, judging from details of their burial.

In the 1960s and early 1970s, Melvin Fowler and a crew from the University of Wisconsin at Milwaukee excavated other pits at Mound 72 containing the bones of sacrificial victims, mostly women. One burial vault held the remains of fifty-three persons, largely female, laid out carefully in two rows. The similarity of their ages, stature, health, and diet suggests that they were deliberately chosen and sacrificed all at once as part of a religious ceremony. In another pit, young adult men and women were buried still lying on the cedar-pole stretchers used to carry them to the site. All had been neatly wrapped in shrouds before being buried directly over a layer of thirty-nine persons who had been executed on the spot, their bodies allowed to drop into the trench, arms and legs askew. These and other ceremonies doubtless involved Cahokian leaders living and dead—the latter including a "bird-man" impersonator whom excavators found buried near the vault, surrounded by retainers and objects connoting religious and political power.

That human sacrifices were made at Cahokia should not be surprising, for almost every society in history has undergone a period when similar things happened, especially at moments when religion, governance, and social inequality were in flux. Despite such troubling evidence of political or religious violence, we suspect that women figured prominently in Cahokian beliefs and society, likely embodying religious beliefs about fertility and the renewal of life (chapter 7).

Back at our Emerald excavation, this interpretation rang true. The bone proved to be that of a young person, probably a woman. Her presence disturbed and upset our students. Some expressed a sense of sorrow that she was alone. Some felt angry with those who might have sacrificed her. Nearly all were unhappy about disturbing her resting place. Also troubling was that a layer of silt covered her remains, the result of a rainstorm that had filled the open pit with sediment before the body was buried. Some students thought this was a sign of disrespect, but we had evidence at Emerald and another nearby site that Cahokians allowed rain or sky spirits to take part in the ceremonial closure of temples, much as had been done in closing this burial. In the end, the burial reminded us that we must put aside personal feelings and try to understand the original intent and meaning of sacrifice, even while considering the concerns of everyone involved in the present, including descendant communities. The burial confirmed the complexity both of Cahokian beliefs and of navigating modern and past ethics.

necklaces, and earspools. Other mound-and-plaza groups were almost certainly special religious complexes, a few of them dedicated to the handling of the dead by ritual specialists.

Between some of the pyramids ran short, elevated causeways, as if walking between the earthworks required special ritual care. Doubtless, other formal avenues graced the city, probably following downtown Cahokia's five-degree-offset grid of mounds and plazas, although researchers have yet to spot them. In the 1800s, visitors to the site still recognized one primary avenue that exited the city to the east, climbed the bluffs above it, and continued as an ancient road for at least fifteen miles until it reached another group of Cahokian pyramids, known as the Emerald site. Along the eastern bluffs stood mortuary scaffolds, charnel houses, and burial mounds.

We believe the founders of Cahokia designed all at once a vast complex of built features—downtown Cahokia, the St. Louis and East St. Louis precincts, outlying pyramids and residential neighborhoods, roadways and spiritually important places of the dead—and then erected them in a series of colossal construction projects starting around the year 1050. Local villages of the preceding Woodland era gave way to the spacious monumentality of the new city. By the late 1000s, so many local farmers and immigrant families had moved to the central Cahokia precinct that its population leaped from the roughly two thousand souls of the underlying Woodland village to around ten thousand, making Cahokia truly a city by the size standards of the earliest ancient cities around the globe. A few thousand more people lived in the newly built precincts of St. Louis and East St. Louis. Farmers and scattered administrators at towns and farmsteads in the surrounding countryside doubled if not trebled the region's total population, to perhaps thirty or forty thousand between about 1050 and 1150.

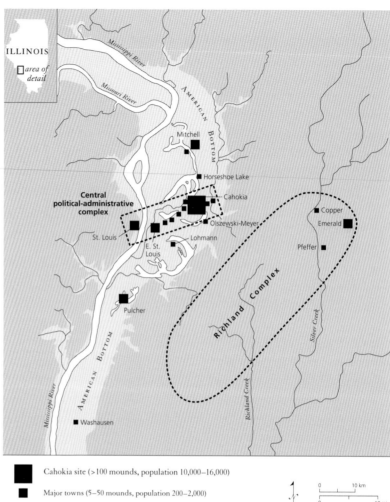

Figure 3.9. Greater Cahokia, showing the capital zone and outlier towns and shrine complexes.

In the countryside around Cahokia proper, farmers lived in isolated farmsteads—a couple of houses surrounded by fields—or in villages. Excavations in at least one such village showed that first- or second-generation immigrants from southern Missouri lived there. Invariably, dispersed in key locations within farming districts were Cahokian religious temples and the homes of priestly or elite families. These ritual and administrative nodes formed part of a huge network that wove greater Cahokia together and linked ordinary villagers to the city, its elites, its ancestors, and its celestial associations. A few important towns outside Cahokia each housed a few hundred people, each with one or more platform mounds and a central

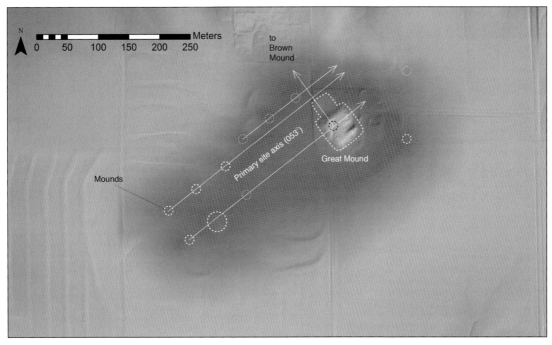

Figure 3.10. Plan of Emerald site mounds and organizational axes based on a LiDAR image. Bold dashed lines are observed circular mounds; thin dashed lines are suspected circular mounds.

plaza featuring upright posts and public or ceremonial buildings.

In some ways, the mounds, plazas, and buildings of these towns in the countryside duplicated the facilities and services offered at Cahokia. But three large, outlying civic and ceremonial complexes, all situated at the edge of a prairie fifteen miles east of Cahokia, appear to have been different. Few people may have lived in them year-round. We believe they served as lunar shrine complexes, built to honor the powers of the earth and sky, especially the moon. There and nearby, people built mounds and plastered temple floors with distinctive yellow and black clay, perhaps denoting the colors of the moon and the night. One of the prairie-edge shrines, the Emerald site, sat on a natural ridge that Cahokians had heavily modified around 1050. The shrine's designers aligned its pyramids with the northernmost point at which the moon rises on the eastern horizon, a once-in-a-generation celestial event that the ancient Hopewell people and the ancestral Pueblo people of Chaco Canyon, New Mexico, also observed. Perhaps before the shrine's rituals, the road connecting Emerald to Cahokia was crowded with devotees.

We think another kind of ritual movement took place occasionally in the city itself. From time to time, Cahokians rebuilt their homes in the same spots but with new orientations—perhaps turned to face a cardinal direction, the rising sun on the summer or winter solstice, a different position of the moon, or the annual appearance of a star or constellation. Undoubtedly they did so largely for religious reasons. But because people had to coordinate and negotiate how and where to build their houses, even home building must have been fraught with politics. One family might be more beholden than another to a leader who identified with the moon. Other leaders, priests, or clans might have identified with the sun, the earth, or beings of the sky. Perhaps entire clans believed themselves descended from these gods. Whatever the practical and political implications of Cahokian society, living in it must have meant working continually to remain in balance with the grander order of the cosmos.

Sometimes the cosmic balance broke down anyway, despite priests' and commoners' best efforts. In the last great public-works project at Cahokia, carried out in the late 1100s, laborers erected a two-mile-long palisade wall, with defensive bastions projecting out every ninety feet, around the core of downtown Cahokia. The Cahokians must have feared an attack against the temples, elite homes, pyramids, and Grand Plaza of this sacred place. Defensive walls also surrounded compounds in the East St. Louis precinct at this time. There, in the 1160s or 1170s, according to radiocarbon dates, much of the standing architecture—hundreds of pole-and-thatch buildings—burned to the ground. Afterward, only religious temples atop platform mounds were rebuilt at East

Mississippian Cosmic Pots

Figure 3.11. Large rim section of a Ramey Incised pot from Cahokia.

Figure 3.12. Ramey Incised rim pieces showing the spiral or "scroll" motif.

The ancient Cahokians' beliefs about the natural order of the universe—their cosmology—took material form in everything from pyramids to cooking pots. Cahokians thought of themselves as occupying the center of a universe alive with cosmic powers, spirits, and deities. The city's planners arranged its innermost ceremonial complex, centered on Monks Mound, the Grand Plaza, and Rattlesnake Causeway, to allow people to experience simultaneously the moving heavens, the powers of the earth, the four winds, and the cycle of life and death. Even pottery vessels, centrally produced at Cahokia and widely distributed across the Mississippian world, served as "cosmic containers."

Rather than depicting scenes, the way Delft china and ancient Greek Attic ware do, Cahokian pots were microcosms—miniature models of the universe. For example, the burnished, black ceremonial jars known as "Ramey Incised" typically featured rim decorations of four repeating rain, wind, thunderbird, or sky god motifs. The most common motif was the Ramey scroll, a spiral that may have represented a sectioned conch shell—an import from the Gulf of Mexico—a wind swirl, or a human dance movement. The vessels might have given their users a feeling of moving between heaven and earth. That is, from the top of the jar, a person reached down from the sky with its sky gods into this world, the black interior of the pot, which held the foodstuffs or liquids of the earth. This pottery sensibility seems to go all the way back to Hopewell times.

St. Louis. Even those stood for only another century or so.

Archaeologists are still unsure whether or not the end of East St. Louis, and ultimately all of greater Cahokia, came about through violent attack, perhaps from the north (chapter 14). This is because ritual burning was common among Mississippian people as a kind of ceremonial closure, sometimes marking the death of a great person. The East St. Louis fire might have been just such a planned ritual event. Either way, it was a harbinger of the end of this peculiarly American medieval experiment in urbanism. Descendants of the Cahokians gradually left the region during the 1200s and 1300s, some of them traveling south down the Mississippi River to live among other Mississippians, others heading west into the southern Great Plains and trans-Mississippi South. Still others, descendants of Cahokia's colonies, converts, allies, and enemies to the north, blended with the Mississippianized Oneota peoples (chapter 5), some of them eventually heading west into the plains.

Thomas E. Emerson is the Illinois state archaeologist, director of the Illinois State Archaeological Survey, Prairie Research Institute, and an adjunct professor of anthropology at the University of Illinois. His research interests range from shipwrecks to the politics and religion of complex societies. Recently he co-edited *Archaic Societies: Diversity and Complexity across the Midcontinent* (2009) and *Late Woodland Societies: Tradition and Transformation in the Midcontinent* (2007).

Michael G. Farkas, an archaeological GIS specialist with the Illinois State Archaeological Survey, has nearly two decades of archaeological geospatial expertise.

Sarah E. Baires is assistant professor of anthropology at Eastern Connecticut State University whose research at Cahokia focuses on the intersection of politics and religion and how the city of Cahokia was constructed.

Figure 4.1. Toltec Mounds, view of Mounds A and B from the northeast. Designers laid out Toltec according to a standard unit of length and oriented the complex to the moon.

Moonwatchers of Cahokia

William F. Romain

For many years, prevailing opinion has held that Cahokia was all about the sun. Even the current display at the Cahokia Mounds interpretive center refers to Cahokia as the "City of the Sun." Undoubtedly, the sun was important to medieval Mississippians. But is it possible that reverence for the sun was only part of the story? Garcilaso de la Vega, a chronicler of the de Soto expedition in the sixteenth century, wrote that southeastern Indians, descendants of the medieval Mississippians, "worship the sun *and* the moon as their principal deities" (my italics). Given this, could it be that veneration of the moon extended back to early Mississippian times, even being incorporated into the design and layout of certain towns? Might Cahokia itself—the flagship city of the medieval Mississippian world—have been connected to the moon? I believe the answer to both questions is yes.

In the 1960s, archaeologist Nelson Reed first recognized that the straight edges of rectangular mounds at Cahokia were typically angled about five degrees east of north. Today we know that a line drawn from the center of Mound 66, or Rattlesnake Mound, along Rattlesnake Causeway and through the Grand Plaza to a small conical mound on Monks Mound's second terrace is also angled five degrees east of north. Parallel axes run from either edge of Mound 72 to Monks Mound (plate 11). The line from the east side of Mound 72, a burial mound, intersects Fox Mound and, together with the Rattlesnake Causeway axis, frames the ramp

leading from ground level to the first terrace of Monks Mound. The line from the west side of Mound 72 passes through a small mound in the southwest corner of the first terrace of Monks Mound.

Lines like these, reaching from a particular spot on the earth's surface toward a given point on the horizon, are called *azimuths*. They are expressed in degrees clockwise from north (which is 0 degrees) around the 360-degree circle of the Earth's horizon. Cahokia's main axis and indeed the entire grid used to lay out the site are oriented along an azimuth of 005 degrees. The city's planners seem to have locked in its axis by tying it redundantly to more than one mound.

But why did the designers choose this seemingly odd orientation? Did they perhaps mean to lay the city out along a true north-south line but make an observational error? Having previously found evidence for solar and lunar alignments at Hopewell sites in Ohio, I wondered whether something similar might explain Cahokia's orientation. I was not the first to look for celestial alignments at greater Cahokia. Tim Pauketat had already discovered that some temple or shrine complexes near the city, such as the Emerald site, had been laid out using lunar directions. But I had the advantage of using new LiDAR imagery for Cahokia, generously provided by the Illinois State Archaeological Survey. I tested for both solar and lunar alignments and discovered several solar ones between a few of the mounds. But

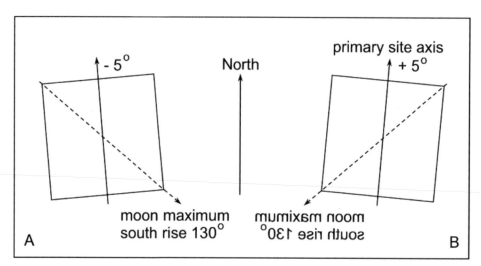

Figure 4.2. *Left*: a square constructed with an azimuth of 130 degrees as its diagonal. *Right*: the same square in mirror image, flipped over its vertical axis.

to my surprise, the city's predominant and most precise alignment, to within one-tenth of a degree, turned out to correspond to the moon—and not quite in a way one might expect. I think the ancient city planners based their site axis on the geometrical use of a line projected from the center of Rattlesnake Mound toward the southernmost point at which the moon rose on the eastern horizon. Let me explain.

Most people are familiar with the way the rising and setting sun moves along the eastern and western horizons, respectively, between the summer and winter solstices. The moon's movement is similar to the sun's, but more complicated. The rising position of the moon moves from north to south and back to north again along the eastern horizon between limits reached once a month. Its setting position does the same thing along the western horizon.

Complicating the situation, the monthly limits themselves oscillate over a cycle of 18.6 years. The range of the moon's rising and setting positions is widest every nineteenth year and narrowest nine and a half years later. Thus, over an 18.6-year cycle, a viewer can observe four extremes for the moon's rising positions—its maximum and minimum north rises and its maximum and minimum south rises—and four comparable extremes for its setting positions. These extremes are sometimes called *lunar standstills*. The exact azimuths at which these rise and set events will be visible on the horizon are a function of date, latitude, horizon elevation, and various correction factors

and are calculated using spherical trigonometry.[1]

By my calculations, in the year 1050 CE and for at least one hundred years on either side of that date, the maximum south moon rise as viewed from the original ground level at Rattlesnake Mound would have occurred at an azimuth of 130 degrees.[2] That is, at its once-in-a-generation south maximum, the moon would have come up at a point 130 degrees clockwise from north, over the bluffs to the southeast.[3] Imagine now that we draw a line from the center of Rattlesnake Mound to that point on the horizon and then construct a square using this 130-degree azimuth as its diagonal. (There are good reasons to believe Cahokia was designed using squares, and I return to that topic later.) The vertical axis of the square necessarily has an azimuth of 355 degrees, or five degrees west of north. That is, it is offset from north in exactly the opposite manner from Cahokia's observed axis. Maybe this is problematical, but I think not.

From what we know of their imagery and the spoken traditions of their descendants, medieval Mississippians probably conceived of the cosmos as composed of opposing dualities: the Above World and the Below World, Earth and Sky, male and female, serpents and falcons, and so on. Perhaps their fascination with dualism originated in a belief that it was interaction between opposites that generated energy, movement, and, in the case of males and females, new life forms. If so, then dualism was part of the generative force of the cosmos, producing fertility and fecundity, matters of vital concern

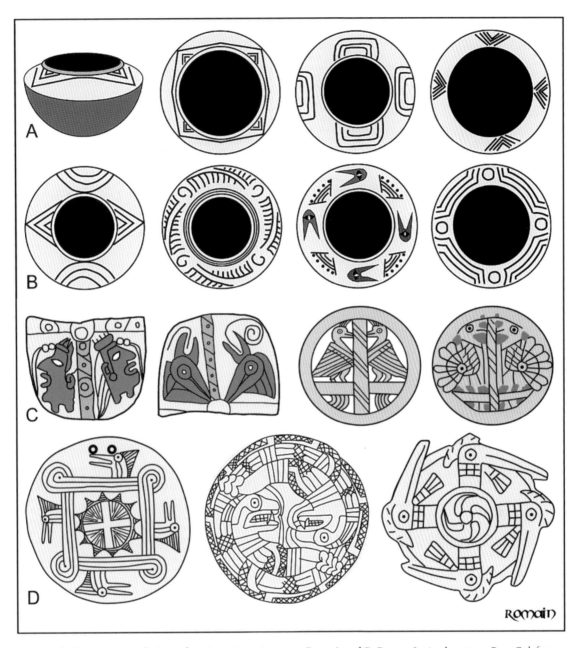

Figure 4.3. Mississippian designs showing mirror imagery. *Rows A and B*: Ramey Incised pottery. *Row C, left to right*: front of a tablet from Cahokia; reverse of the same table; shell gorget from Etowah, Georgia; shell gorget from the Hixon site, Tennessee. *Row D, left to right*: gorget reportedly found in Mississippi; the Issaquena disk; gorget from Spiro Mounds, Oklahoma.

to people dependent on successful harvests. Complementary duality found expression in many Mississippian objects and designs, often through the use of mirror images, in which the reflected image is an exact duplicate of the first image, but reversed.

Cahokians well understood mirror imagery, as can be seen in the designs on their Ramey Incised pots. Mississippian people elsewhere in the

Southeast made similar vessels. After studying the contexts in which excavators have found such pots, as well as the symbolism of their incised designs, Tom Emerson and Tim Pauketat made a convincing case that Ramey Incised pottery had religious importance and incorporated ideas about the nature of the cosmos. When a Ramey Incised vessel is viewed from the top down, the design field along its shoulder invariably consists of motifs arranged in mirror image relationships.

Other examples of Mississippian mirror imagery decorate small etched stone tablets found at Cahokia and shell gorgets—carved ornaments hung from a necklace or choker—uncovered at other Mississippian towns. Some of the designs on these pieces show two human heads mirroring each other, or two woodpecker heads, or two turkeys. More complicated designs each depict two sets of mirroring woodpecker heads. On a sandstone object known as the Issaquena disk, found in Issaquena County, Mississippi, an artist reversed two rattlesnakes both vertically and horizontally.

The mirror image concept may explain Cahokia's city plan. If we flip our lunar-derived constructed square over its vertical axis, the result is a complementary square with its vertical axis oriented five degrees east of north—just like Cahokia's primary axis. We can now see the primary site axis, Rattlesnake Mound, Rattlesnake Causeway, Monks Mound, Fox Mound, and indeed the city's entire grid as oriented to an azimuth derived from the moon's maximum south rise.

Is this inference too far-fetched? I recognize that the prospect of North America's premier medieval city being oriented to a flipped lunar azimuth might raise skeptical eyebrows. But I think there are two plausible explanations for why the Cahokians reversed a perfectly good lunar azimuth and then built their city in what amounts to a backward manner. One explanation involves sky watching and the way directions seemingly reverse when one changes perspective between earth and sky. This concept is well known to anyone who has ever held a star map up to the sky and tried to read it. The following exercise shows what I mean.

Imagine you are standing at the base of Rattlesnake Mound, looking east toward the bluffs about two miles away. Hold figure 4.4 out in front of you, parallel to the ground, with east pointing away from you and the moon's maximum south rise duly pointing to about your two o'clock position. This represents the earth view of things, the same view you would use if you were drawing an azimuth on the flat surface of the earth. Next, take the book, turn it upside-down, and hold it

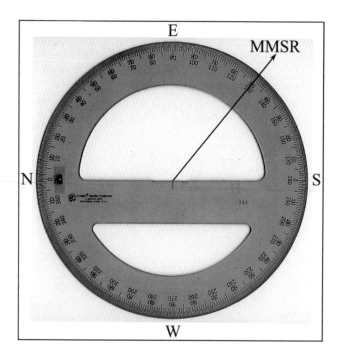

Figure 4.4. Demonstration showing earth and sky views of the moon's maximum south rise azimuth.

over your head, parallel to the sky. Now, east is facing toward your rear, west is to your front, and the moon's maximum south rise is pointing to your four o'clock position, over your right shoulder. This represents the sky view and is the conceptual equivalent of the flipped imagery already described—reflecting, in this case, the complementary, opposite relationship between earth and sky, referenced to the moon.

The second explanation relates to the fact that many American Indian tribes across the eastern woodlands considered the Land of the Dead to be the reverse of This World. When it was daytime in This World, it was nighttime in the Land of the Dead. What was right-side up in This World was upside-down in the Land of the Dead. Perhaps the planners who laid out Cahokia using a flipped lunar azimuth were steeped in this concept of reversed cosmological realms. In This World, the city's lunar-derived grid pointed in one direction; in the Otherworld, it pointed in the mirror-image direction. Neither direction was "correct," for both depended on the viewer's perspective.

I should add that the use of diagonals through squares to establish alignments to celestial events

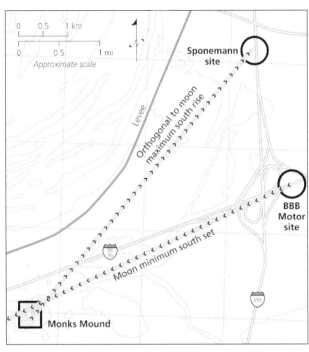

Figure 4.5. Lunar relationships between Monks Mound and the Sponemann and BBB Motor sites.

had precedent in the eastern woodlands, as documented for the earlier Hopewell culture in south-central Ohio (150 BCE–400 CE). The designers of many Hopewell sites, including Mound City, Hopeton, Seip, and the namesake Hopewell site itself, used diagonal sightlines through square earthworks to establish celestial alignments. Similarly, the alignment of sites to lunar standstill events finds precedent among the Hopewell, most notably at the Newark and High Bank sites. So although the alignment of Cahokia to the moon using a flipped azimuth is unique, it is not without conceptual support in both Mississippian iconography and earlier Hopewell earthworks.

Why might Cahokians have wanted to tie the orientation of their city to the moon rather than the sun or some other celestial body or event? For Native peoples of the eastern woodlands, the moon has long played an important role in tracking human, plant, animal, and cosmic rhythms. Many tribes in historic times scheduled important ceremonial events, feasts, and other activities according to dates reckoned by lunar months.

Perhaps more important, an explanation for Cahokia's lunar orientation may lie in the symbolic

association of the moon with an entity known as Earth Mother. The Earth Mother concept is widely documented for tribes across eastern North America. In the indigenous Midwest and South, people traditionally associate Earth Mother, the bringer of maize, with plant growth, fertility, reproduction, birth, and death. She is also linked to water, serpents, the Below World, and, most significantly for us, the moon. In many eastern North American mythologies, including those of the Shawnees, Iroquois, Hurons, Pawnees, Caddos, Wichitas, Arikaras, and Ojibwas, Earth Mother—also known as Old Woman, Corn Mother, and Grandmother—either has lunar associations or is a lunar goddess.

In the immediate vicinity of Cahokia, archaeologists have discovered female figurines in places with strong connections to the moon. Pieces of three figurines come from the Sponemann site, which sits only two and a half miles northeast of Monks Mound—on an azimuth perpendicular to the azimuth of the moon's maximum south rise. At the nearby BBB Motor site, excavators found another two female figurines. Viewed from that site, the moon appears to set into Monks Mound on the date of its minimum south position.

In chapter 7, Tom Emerson makes a convincing case that Mississippians associated such figurines with themes of fertility, serpents, and plant foods—all attributes of the Earth Mother goddess. What we have, then, are two satellite Cahokian temple sites, each yielding female figurines representing fertility, spatially connected to the moon through Monks Mound, the most visually impressive feature of Cahokia. If Cahokia's designers sought to incorporate symbolism invoking plentiful harvests and prolific fertility, then what better way to do so than to consecrate the entire city to the Earth Mother–Moon Goddess by connecting the city's primary axis and major mounds to her nighttime sky manifestation?

Another line of support for the idea that Cahokia's orientation is lunar derived comes from Mound 72. Its long axis lies on an azimuth of 307 degrees, pointing precisely toward the moon's maximum north set, the conceptual opposite of the moon's maximum south rise. Even more striking, excavators in the 1960s and 1970s uncovered the remains of more than 260 persons, including dozens of sacrificed women, in mass graves beneath Mound 72. The orientations of all the mass burials can be accounted for by simple iterations of the flipped square concept.

Under the mound, excavators also found the wall trenches of a pole-and-thatch temple or charnel house, probably the place where many of the Mound 72 dead were processed. As my measurements show, it turns out that the diagonal axis of the charnel house is aligned to the moon's maximum south rise along the same azimuth so vital for all of Cahokia. A lunar association is appropriate for a charnel house; indigenous descendants commonly associate the moon with the night and the realm of the dead. And because Mound 72 sits along one of the site's principal parallel axes, the alignment of its charnel house further links Cahokia directly to the moon.

Some researchers have suggested that the Cahokians sacrificed and buried people in Mound 72 to act as servants or retainers in the afterlife for important leaders buried nearby, to display power or disposable wealth, or to serve as offerings in rituals celebrating the deaths of Cahokian enemies. An alternative explanation, more consistent with my lunar findings, is that in return for the offering of these persons' life forces and vitality to the Earth Mother–Moon Goddess, Cahokians hoped the goddess or the powers of the Lower World would bestow on them abundant harvests and prolific fertility. The late archaeologist Robert L. Hall proposed a similar idea years ago, suggesting that the Mound 72 sacrifices were made to the Corn Goddess. Certainly, sacrifices and offerings in anticipation of reciprocal gifts are known for many cultures around the world, throughout human history.

I believe a reciprocal relationship existed between the Cahokian community and the Earth Mother–Moon Goddess. If so, then perhaps Cahokians believed that the Mound 72 sacrifices would help assure the community's continued success.

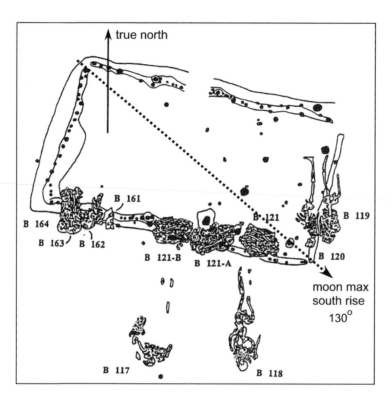

Figure 4.6. Plan of the temple or charnel house under Mound 72, showing wall trenches, post holes (black circles), burials placed over the south and east walls, and the building's lunar alignment.

Once the city's planners had decided how to incorporate the moon's maximum south alignment into the layout of Cahokia, their likely next step was to situate mounds around the edges of idealized squares oriented to the primary site axis (plate 12). Some such squares became leveled plazas—most notably, the Grand Plaza. Once planners had committed themselves to the design square concept, not every mound had to be rigidly positioned exactly on a predetermined survey line to successfully convey the general idea. Nor did every mound have to be built at the same time. But as plate 12 shows, the placement of pyramids along the edges of squares was in no way coincidental.

Nor were the sizes of the squares accidental; they were based on multiples of a standard unit of measurement. In 1987, P. Clay Sherrod and Martha Ann Rolingson, while studying linear distances between mounds at Cahokia and several other Mississippian towns, proposed that the towns were laid out in units of 1,045 meters, or about 3,428 feet. (Because archaeologists use metric

H. Roe 2013

Figure 4.7. Author's conceptualization of the reciprocal relationship between the Cahokian community and the Earth Mother–Moon Goddess. The depiction of the goddess is based on archaeologically recovered Cahokian figurines.

measurements, I follow suit here.) Moreover, the 1,045-meter unit was a multiple of a unit 47.5 meters in length—namely, it was 22 × 47.5 meters. Because it was based on their study of the Toltec site in Arkansas, Sherrod and Rolingson called the 47.5-meter length the "Toltec module."

For Cahokia, each side of the largest square shown in plate 12 measures the full 1,045 meters long. Each side of the second largest square—the one defining the Grand Plaza—measures 522.5 meters, or

11 × 47.5 meters, exactly half the size of the large square. North of the Grand Plaza, the east and west design squares were meant to be one-quarter the size of the Grand Plaza. Not only that, but the east and west squares are separated from each other by a distance of about 522.5 meters, again the multiple of eleven times the Toltec module. North of Monks Mound is a rectangle bisected by the primary site axis and formed from two overlapping squares, each the same size as the east and west squares.

Monks Mound has changed in size over the centuries, first as the Cahokians enlarged and refurbished it and later as it eroded, slumped, and underwent repair. But I suspect its designers originally modeled its dimensions on a rectangle having its long sides equal to the sides of the squares east and west of the mound and its short sides equal to one-half the length of the north rectangle (plate 12). The dimensions of many smaller mounds, such as Mounds 5, 42, 48, 66, and 72, are lesser multiples of the 1,045-meter unit.

Just as the use of celestially aligned azimuths as diagonals of squares finds precedent in Hopewell sites, so the use of a standard unit of length finds precedent in earlier sites. One example is Toltec Mounds, in present-day Arkansas, about three hundred miles southwest of Cahokia. Toltec dates from about 700 to 1050 CE. Its designers not only used the Toltec module in its layout but also oriented the site to the moon. Besides the several solar alignments between Toltec mounds that Rolingson and Sherrod discovered in the 1980s, I find that Toltec's short axis is oriented to the moon's maximum south rise—the same event to which Cahokians referenced their city plan. Indeed, all eighteen mounds inside the site's perimeter walls are situated on a grid tied to the moon's maximum south rise.

Archaeological evidence indicates that earthwork construction at Toltec Mounds ended around 1050 CE, just at the time of Cahokia's "Big Bang." Considering this timing and Toltec's relative proximity to Cahokia, several Mississippian experts believe that at least some Toltec site people migrated to what was to become Cahokia. I agree and would add that these immigrants probably brought with them sophisticated knowledge of astronomy, geometry, and mensuration, the products of hundreds of years of sky watching, site design, and mound building. I think it likely that the designers of Cahokia incorporated and elaborated on that knowledge.

Alignments to the heavens connected Cahokians to the cyclical flow of time, brought the city into harmony with the cosmos, and created links to the forces that affected the community. Geometry gave shape to the formless and established relationships between things while measurement lent sequential and predictable order. The dualistic nature of the cosmos was represented at

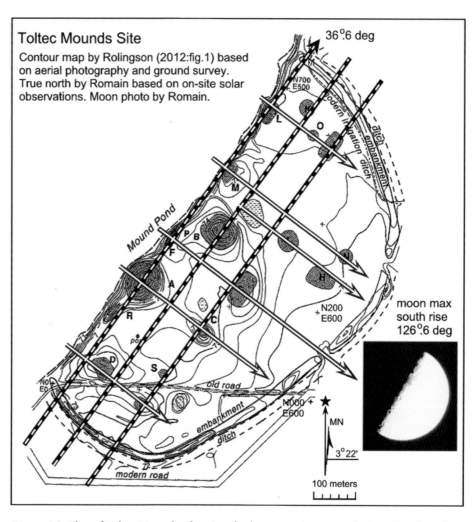

Figure 4.8. Plan of Toltec Mounds, showing the lunar maximum south rise azimuth and the lunar grid on which the site's mounds were laid out.

multiple scales. Of central concern was the interplay between life and death and the way those matters related to fertility and successful harvests, on which the community's survival depended.

From the sacrificed women in Mound 72, lunar alignments, ritual deposits, satellite temples, figurines, and even broken pottery, it is clear that Cahokian design principles, earthworks, objects, and people were deeply intertwined with the cosmos. For Cahokians, what we call "sacred" probably lay all around, at all times, and formed an essential part of life. Their religion was a lived experience that infused the senses at many levels, guided thinking, and, through action, resulted in the unprecedented phenomenon we know as Cahokia.

Acknowledgments

I thank Tim Pauketat and Susan Alt for inviting me to contribute to this volume. I greatly appreciate comments Tim offered on earlier drafts of the chapter. My design squares are iterations of Warren Wittry and Melvin Fowler's explications concerning Cahokian plazas. Thomas Emerson and John Kelly enlightened my understanding of Cahokian quadrilateralism and cosmic duality. Several insights regarding the Earth Mother–Moon Goddess originated with Emerson. And without the LiDAR data provided by Tom Emerson and Mike Farkas, I could not have written the chapter. I also thank the Newark Earthworks Center, Ohio State University, for continued support of my LiDAR research. I am solely responsible for the content of this chapter.

Notes

1. Relevant azimuths for 1000 CE from the base of Rattlesnake Mound, corrected for measured horizon elevations and lower edge of the sun and moon: moon maximum north rise, 53.4°; moon maximum south rise, 130.07°; moon minimum north rise, 67.4°; moon minimum south rise, 115.6°; moon maximum north set, 307.1°; moon maximum south set, 231.2°; moon minimum north set, 293.3°; moon minimum south set, 245.4°; summer solstice rise, 59.7°; summer solstice set, 300.9°; winter solstice rise, 121.8°; winter solstice set, 239.3°.

2. Maximum moon south rise of 130.07° is calculated for 1000 CE, map-measured horizon elevation corrected for refraction, lower limb tangency, and parallax, where horizontal distance between backsight and foresight = 11,683 feet and vertical distance = 247 feet, which includes estimated foresight tree height of 80 feet, for a corrected horizon elevation of 2.02°. It is also possible, but less likely, that Cahokia's major axis was established by using the moon's maximum south set rather than its maximum south rise. That is, a square having its major axis oriented to 005 degrees, like the Cahokia site axis, has as its diagonal an azimuth of 230 degrees, which is 1.2 degrees off from the moon's maximum south set azimuth of 231.2 degrees. Although this alignment is less precise than the posited moon maximum south rise, it is simpler.

3. A small knoll stands where the moon's maximum south rise sightline intersects the bluff. No record exists that anything has been found at this location, but neither is there any record that anyone ever looked. Today the knoll is part of someone's backyard.

William F. Romain, who received his doctorate from the University of Leicester, England, is a research associate with the Newark Earthworks Center at Ohio State University and an advisor to the Heartland Earthworks Conservancy. His interests include the origins of religion, cognitive neuroscience, archaeoastronomy, and pre-Columbian American Indian cultures. He is the author of *Mysteries of the Hopewell: Astronomers, Geometers, and Magicians of the Eastern Woodlands* (2000) and *Shamans of the Lost World: A Cognitive Approach to the Prehistoric Religion of the Ohio Hopewell* (2009).

Figure 5.1. Marisa Cummings with her son, Darius, and daughter, Nia, enjoying themselves at a dance.

An Umonhon Perspective

Marisa Miakonda Cummings

My name is Marisa Cummings. My Umonhon (Omaha) name is Miakonda, or Moon Power, "the one who gets her power from the full moon." I belong to the TeCinde, or Buffalo Tail clan, of the Sky people. My father is the late Mike Cummings. His Umonhon name is TeNugaNaTide, or Stampeding Buffalo. My grandmother is Eunice Walker. Her Umonhon name is TeCinde Wa'u, or Buffalo Tail Clan Woman. In my teachings, this is how we introduce ourselves, so you know who I am and where I come from. It is my identity as an Umonhon woman. I am in no way a cultural expert. I do not speak on behalf of my people; I can speak only on behalf of myself, drawing on the teachings I have received and on my own thoughts and understandings.

Growing up I heard a great deal about Cahokia from my father. He was an "urban" Indian, born on the reservation at an Indian Health Service hospital and raised in Sioux City, Iowa. A first-generation college student in the 1970s, he graduated with a bachelor's degree from Morningside College and then earned a master's degree from Iowa State University. He was part of a new generation of educated Natives growing up in the era of self-determination. Cahokia signified and affirmed that we were more than wandering savages. It gave us pride in the fact that our people built cities and created trade networks that baffled

anthropologists. So, when I was a young Umonhon girl being taught about her identity, my father used Cahokia as a reference of cultural pride and identity. The interest in Cahokia he inspired in me spurred my studies at the University of Iowa and my research into the Umonhon people and our past.

For Umonhon people, as for other Native groups, being Umonhon involves our interactions within our tribal community. These interactions are based on a clan system that confers on us specific duties and responsibilities and also dictates certain interactions with other clans. Equally important is our identity in relation to other communities. I tend always to be aware of how we are similar to and how we are different from those communities in regard to language, family interactions, ceremonies, and other cultural exchanges.

As Umonhon people, we know that we come from a larger group called Dhegiha. In the past, we identified as this group of people and intermarried within it in specific clanship marriages. These relationships were clearly defined and organized. I use the term *relationships* because I was raised to think of our Dhegiha relatives—the Poncas, Osages, Quapaws, and Kaws—as our brother and sister tribes, closely related. We are also closely related to the Iowa, Otoe, and Missouri people. Our tribal entities did not exist in a vacuum.

We were constantly exchanging cultural and material property through trade. We were constantly "making relatives" through adoption ceremonies and marriages. We did not act independently of one another but, rather, interdependently. Our teachings tell us that we cannot exist independently as humans; we need one another to survive and thrive.

I do not wish to create an image of a Native paradise. We also warred with one another and raided other groups for resources and women. Contrary to outsiders' beliefs, this was done out of necessity for the people. Among the Umonhon, there are two types of warfare: to defend the women and children and to attack. In times of socioeconomic hardship, it was sometimes necessary to take resources from other tribes for survival. Often the same tribes that warred were the very tribes that came together for sociocultural gatherings throughout the year. These gatherings involved social dances and doings, encouraged cultural exchange and trade, and incorporated our spiritual practices. Some people compare the contemporary powwow to this type of gathering, for a powwow is an occasion to meet people from different tribal groups, sing, dance, and enjoy oneself in a good way.

Judging from oral tradition and my understanding of who we are as Umonhon people, I believe we were not residents of Cahokia proper. We maintained our mound-building status to the north, as a suburb of sorts. Some of our Dhegiha relatives separated from us at the Mississippi River and went to the south. It is possible that these groups, the Osages and Quapaws ("downstream people"), had a relationship with Cahokia, but I cannot speak for them. The idea of a city of mounds would not have been unknown to us, though, because our trade

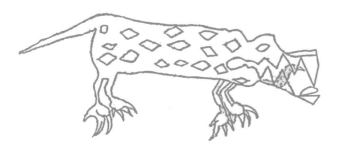

networks across Turtle Island (North America) were extensive.

As Umonhon people, we tell our history through oral tradition. One oral method of historical record keeping is through song. An elder woman relative, a member of the Honga clan, recently told me about a song we have that tells the story of Umonhon women being stolen by Pawnees and sacrificed in the Morningstar ceremony. Some Dhegiha people believe the Pawnee Morningstar ceremony came from Cahokia. The song tells of an Umonhon woman being tied up so that her arms are spread out while Pawnees shoot arrows at her and blood falls from the wounds. It is my understanding this ceremony was practiced at Cahokia and followed the groups as they moved north.

From both oral tradition and anthropological and archaeological evidence, we know that the Umonhon came from a city built south of present-day Sioux Falls, South Dakota, before European contact. This city extends across the Iowa and South Dakota borders and is today composed of mounds and effigies. Later, white inhabitants called the site Blood Run. From about 1500 to 1700 CE, it was inhabited by so-called Oneota people, primarily the Omaha-Ponca, Otoe, and Ioway. The city was a center of trade in pipestone for disk pipes as well as pipestone tablets. The Ioway traded these tablets into Ho-Chunk country to the east. On a 1718 map, French traders saw a road that was already established and called it the "Road of the Voyagers." The French used this road in their travels for trade. The existence of the road again illustrates Indian peoples' interdependence and the relationships we Umonhon had with our relative tribes. The site now called Blood Run was also a place of cultural and ceremonial exchange comparable to Cahokia, but without a fortification.

When viewing Native artwork, I tend to look for commonalities in designs and in the meanings behind the designs. For instance, I see links to the present in the "Ramey" symbolism of Cahokian and Oneota pots (chapter 3). The pottery beakers found at Cahokia that I call "coffee mugs" are also very interesting to me. The black mug illustrated in plate 2 appears to have a wind design engraved into it, and the yellow mug, a four-directions design.

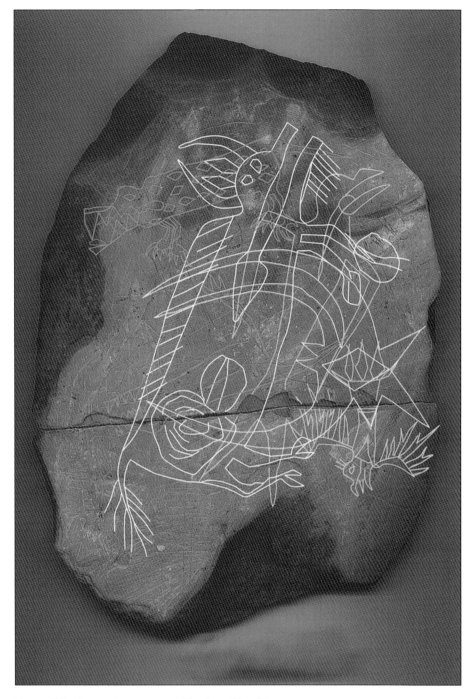

Figure 5.2. Engraved pipestone tablet from Blood Run.

held a heavily caffeinated, imported black tea—a sort of coffee on steroids—I instantly thought of our Umoⁿhoⁿ coffee. Native people tend to make coffee very strong. In Umoⁿhoⁿ, we call coffee *makoⁿ cabe*. *Makoⁿ* means medicine. *Cabe* means black. In essence, Black Medicine.

That Mississippian temples, pyramids, and whole site layouts were aligned to the moon (chapter 4) is not surprising to me. I would think that this alignment had something to do with women. In my Umoⁿhoⁿ teachings, women are directly associated with the moon and her energy. The moon is also associated with water, which is life. When women are pregnant, their bellies fill with water, and the baby lives in water. Our bellies become big and round, like the moon. Women are life givers. Many Umoⁿhoⁿ women have clan names connected with the moon. I was told that Umoⁿhoⁿ women once had full-moon ceremonies for the water, but unfortunately these are not practiced among us today.

In the teachings I received, the Umoⁿhoⁿ

The four directions on the mug are more representative of a Lakota-Dakotah-Nakotah four-directions symbol than the Umoⁿhoⁿ-Ponca four-directions sign, which looks like a circle with an X in the middle. The yellow mug also has etchings that are similar to yet different from those seen on pottery from Blood Run. When I was told that these cups once

are divided into Sky people and Earth people. Each has specific duties. Hoⁿgasheⁿu (Earth) people take care of the land and the people. Iⁿshta Cunda (Sky) people are spiritual people. During Mepa Hoⁿga (First Thunders), when the first thunderstorm comes in, we hold ceremonies, for this is our new year, a new beginning and a renewal of life. Our

Thunder clan people take care of these rites. My father taught me that at this time the thunderbird comes, bringing both life and death. He shoots lightning from his eyes. He wakes up all the insects, snakes, and underground animals so they can awaken the Earth. Everything turns green with the life-giving, sacred rain.

When I think of our ancient ones or ancestors, I feel a great sense of connection to them, but also disconnection at the same time. I am eternally grateful for my grandmother, who is always teaching and loving. I am also thankful to my father for taking the time to talk to our elders and ask the important questions he did, so he could pass the sacred teachings on to me. I am by no means an expert, but I inherited my father's passion for understanding and knowledge, and I am always learning. Although my father is no longer with us, I continue to do my best to learn in a respectful way. My grandmother has been the foundation of our family's teachings. Eighty years old as I write this in 2013, she remembers a time much different from the one I know, and she tells her stories elegantly. When I talk to my children about who we are as Umonhon people and about our teachings, I tell them the same stories over and over, so they, too, will retain this information and pass it on.

We present-day Umonhon did not witness life as it was hundreds or thousands of years ago. We can only take the teachings of our elders and correlate oral tradition with contemporary anthropology and archaeology to gain a better understanding of who we were and, even more important, who we still are. So long as our people make the sacrifice to learn the language of our elders, so long as our songs tell our stories, so long as oral tradition is handed down, so long as we dance our dances, we as a people are alive.

Acknowledgments

I would like to say *wibthahan* (thank you) to all my Umonhon relatives in each of the four hills. May we continue to honor our ancestors by maintaining our traditions, culture, and language. A special thank-you to my *konha* (grandmother) Eunice Walker, who is the oldest TeCinde woman and leads by example to show us what an elder should be like. A special thank-you to my late father, Michael Cummings (TeNugaNaTide), for all his sacrifices made for the people: your teachings were not in vain. A special thank-you to my little granddaughter, Wynema Morris (Honga), for reminding me of the rich historical documentation that exists through our songs. A special thank-you to my dear friend Dale Henning, who has shown me a genuine spirit and allowed me to trust an anthropologist. A special thank-you to the Umonhon Society for serving as a vehicle of traditional knowledge and sharing; may our vision of a cultural renaissance come to fruition in our lifetime. *Gatega* (I am done) *Ewithai wongithe* (All my relations).

Marisa Miakonda Cummings is the director of public relations and institutional advancement for Little Priest Tribal College in Winnebago, Nebraska. An advocate for tribal colleges and universities, she also serves as a board member for the Ho-Chunk Community Development Corporation and is involved in the preservation and protection of Good Earth State Park at Blood Run, as well as in archaeological and traditional research. She is a member of the Umonhon Society, which is dedicated to preserving the Umonhon way of life by upholding traditional values, language, and culture.

Figure 6.1. *Mode of Tilling and Planting in Indigenous Florida*, engraving made by Theodor de Bry after a 1564 painting by Jacques Le Moyne.

Mississippians and Maize

Six

Amber M. VanDerwarker

On a sunny afternoon in early May in the year 100 BCE, a woman plants her spring garden with squashes and an array of seed-bearing plants that also grow wild around her village—goosefoot, amaranth, maygrass, little barley, erect knotweed, marsh elder, and sunflower. Her husband had cleared the small garden plot the previous year by cutting down and then burning the natural vegetation on it. Now the woman casts her seeds over the ground by hand. She has always done things this way and cannot imagine making many changes to her garden.

Still, she is curious about a new plant her neighbors have been discussing. Last season, her family attended a festival two valleys to the west at which they traded their baskets and deerskin bags for bone hairpins and grinding stones. Roasting along the edge of the dance grounds was something the woman had neither seen nor smelled before, a food she heard someone call "maize." When she tasted it and sighed with pleasure, the woman next to her smiled and told her it was a powerful food, a food of the gods, and that her own son had been blessed to have been given some seeds by an influential family in a southern valley.

Back in her garden, the woman wipes sweat from her brow and reaches for the pouch tied around her neck. She empties it into her hand and counts fourteen maize seeds—a gift from her new friend at last year's festival. As she plants the seeds, she chants a brief prayer to the gods to help them grow. If the plants yield fruit, she will roast and serve it at the local summer festival as part of the annual harvest ceremony. Her clan is hosting the festival this year, and serving a food of the gods will bring them much prestige.

Eleven hundred years later, this woman's many-times-great-granddaughter finishes the easy task of planting her home garden. After quickly hoeing the small plot, she broadcasts seeds from many native plants, just as her ancestor once did. Her family will eat some of the harvested greens and seeds raw, use some to season and cook with, and process some of the seeds into oil or flour.

Now the woman moves on to a more strenuous job in a bigger field. She swings her stone-bladed garden hoe and digs it into the soil. On her back, her infant daughter sleeps in a sling. When the woman finishes this last row, she'll trade her hoe for a digging stick, jabbing holes in which she'll plant her seeds—here, exclusively maize and squash. Her mother and sister work alongside her on adjacent rows, for this is her family's field, passed down through her mother's line. In a few years, her daughter will join in preparing and planting the field. The woman has always done things this way and cannot imagine a time when fields and gardens were not planted as she plants them now.

Cahokia's monumental architecture, its dense urban population, the spread of Mississippian religious and political power throughout the American South—what fueled it all was the humble field crop

Figure 6.2. *Industry of the Floridians in Depositing Their Crops in the Public Granary*, engraving made by Theodor de Bry after a 1564 painting by Jacques Le Moyne.

maize, or Indian corn. My fictional agricultural experimenter would have been among the first to grow maize in the central Mississippi Valley. Afterward, the crop took hold there only slowly, over many centuries. Not until as late as 800 CE did villagers everywhere in the region at last make maize a standard part of their husbandry. And even so, chemical analyses of human bones confirm that the plant remained relatively unimportant in their diet.

Then, between 800 and 1050, the picture began to change. The human population of the central valley grew substantially, partly through natural reproduction and partly because of an influx of immigrants during the 900s and early 1000s. Instead of moving their small hamlets about the landscape as they had long done, people began to settle down in permanent villages. They also began planting a great deal more maize and relying on it more heavily for their livelihood. By the 900s, maize had become a cornerstone of the subsistence economy. Archaeologists find charred kernels and

cobs everywhere in the debris around the remnants of Late Woodland houses.

Why did maize became a staple crop in Late Woodland times? The answer starts with human population growth. When people of the central Mississippi Valley first adopted maize, their time-tested horticultural practices, supplemented by hunting, fishing, and collecting wild plants, afforded sufficient food for a relatively small and fairly stable population. These people were willing to add maize to their larders, but they saw little reason to reshape their lives around an untried food.

By around 900, though, residents of the region had been growing in number for a thousand years since maize first appeared. Perhaps there were more hungry mouths to feed now than the old mode of subsistence could satisfy. And by now, local farmers had been adapting maize to their environment for centuries. No doubt they experimented with soil conditions, learned to alternately crop the land and let it lie fallow, and improved the quality of their

Garden Hoes

Before the beginning of the Medieval Warm Period, a few peoples of the central Mississippi Valley tilled their gardens with modest, ground limestone or chipped stone hoe blades. Most groups simply broadcast seeds by hand after slash-and-burn field preparation. The Cahokians and other Mississippians, in contrast, manufactured or imported many thousands of standardized, chipped stone hoe blades (chapter 13). Mississippian farmers' increasing use of hoe technology reflects their more intensive planting of fields, together with a decrease in field rotation and the shortening of fallow cycles.

Figure 6.3. Replica of a hoe blade chipped from Mill Creek chert, lashed onto a wooden handle.

plants by selectively sowing seeds from only the best specimens. The people of the Mississippi Valley had become maize experts. It made good sense for them to devote more land to cornfields and to plant those fields more densely, even if doing so demanded more labor and left less time for hunting and gathering.

With the transformation of a large village east of the river into the new city of Cahokia around 1050 came a dramatic wave of population growth, and with it, an enormous need for more maize. Within a few decades, the population of the city proper leaped from around fifteen hundred to more than ten thousand people. Cahokia's size must have outstripped its ability to feed itself; it now needed surplus food from surrounding rural farms.

To obtain this food, the leaders of Cahokia—and those of other capital towns later—probably made a strategic economic decision that catalyzed even greater intensification of maize farming. They began to tax their people, requiring that farmers deliver to them a portion of their yearly maize crop. Archaeologists call this type of tax payment "tribute." To provide tribute without going hungry, farmers had to grow more food than they needed to feed their families. Leaders could use this surplus to feed the workers who toiled to build pyramids, temples, and other public and elite edifices. The surplus could also support artisans and elite families who did not produce their own food.

Mississippian elites might have exerted not only political power in pursuit of food but also religious power or persuasion. By studying the Mississippians' worldview as expressed in imagery, rituals, and monumental spaces, archaeologists have demonstrated that they associated maize with concepts of fertility and renewal. Some researchers have even suggested that maize took a millennium to become a staple food in the central Mississippi Valley because people saw it as a ritual plant, not a primary food source. If indeed maize entered the eastern woodlands as a "food of the gods," then perhaps the medieval intensification of maize farming came about partly because of a religious mandate from leaders. Couching an order to grow more corn in religious terms might have given leaders the legitimacy they needed to convince their people to comply and agree to levies of tribute.

As Cahokia reached its peak of political and economic complexity between 1100 and 1200 CE,

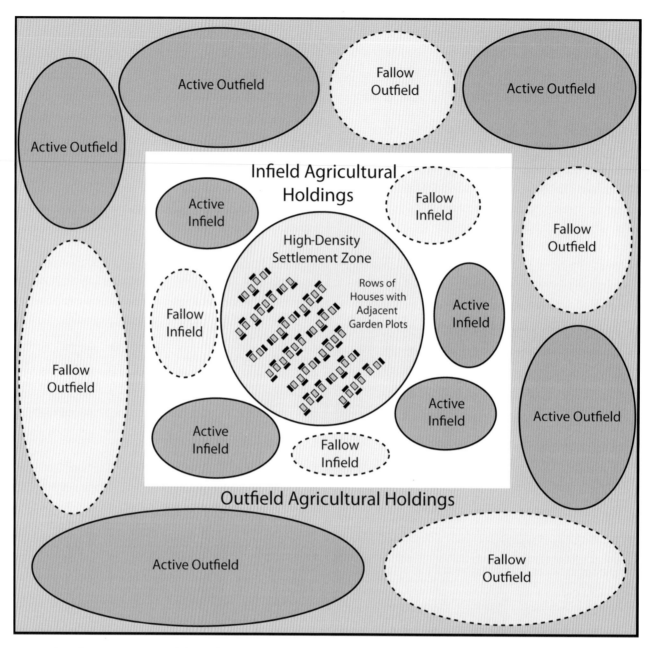

Figure 6.4. The Mississippian infield-outfield agricultural system.

maize production jumped once more. At the same time—and not coincidentally—the city's estimated population dropped by half. Presumably, many residents moved into outlying rural areas. The explanation for these related developments lies in agricultural efficiency. A relatively dense, urban population requires more farmland than is available in or adjacent to its city. Cahokia's residents would have had to cultivate distant fields (outfields) to supplement harvests from their adjacent fields (infields). Tending fields both near and far

would have cost dearly in labor and travel time. By relocating to smaller settlements in the countryside, farmers could reduce their travel time, because most of their fields would now be infields around their new home. Even though they still had to deliver tribute to Cahokia, incurring transportation costs, overall travel time probably diminished. As a result, farming efficiency increased, and so did productivity as farmers grew more maize per unit of land by investing more time and labor in their rural infields.

The rise of Cahokia set the stage for the intensification of maize farming in other parts of the Mississippian world, but Mississippianized people did not follow suit everywhere in the same way, at the same time, or for the same reasons. For example, at the political capital of Moundville in Alabama, maize intensification appears to have preceded the emergence of Mississippian-style political complexity, which took place there in the 1100s. As at Cahokia, surplus maize might have been a key factor leading to the development of inequality and the rise of leaders at Moundville. Just northwest of Moundville, however, at the site of Lubbub Creek in east-central Mississippi, the timing of maize intensification and political development was reversed: the establishment of a political hierarchy preceded intensification. And to the south of Cahokia, scant evidence exists that maize was ever more than a supplemental food resource for the people of the Coles Creek culture of Mississippi and Louisiana before they were "Mississippianized," in large part by Cahokia. In this southern region, monumental constructions and centralized communities had developed by 700 CE in the absence of corn agriculture (chapter 2).

These few examples show that peoples of the medieval Midwest and South followed more than one path to adopting the Mississippian way of life and its economic underpinnings. Arguably, the strategies used by aspiring Cahokian leaders were the most successful, considering the staggering difference in size between Cahokia's territory and the smaller realms of its Mississippian contemporaries and successors. Harnessing surplus maize was key to funding important public and ritual events in and around Cahokia, and those events in turn were critical for integrating elites and commoners from both urban and rural settlements. In short, public ceremony and spectacle at Cahokia, founded on a maize economy, promoted solidarity while cementing status differences. Ultimately, it was a constellation of environmental factors (such as population growth and the development of improved strains of maize), economic decisions (such as decisions to demand tribute in the form of surplus maize), and religious beliefs (such as a belief that maize was a gift from the gods, symbolizing fertility and renewal) that allowed medieval Cahokian leaders to harness the potential of maize toward enlarging and enriching their dominion.

Amber M. VanDerwarker is an associate professor at the University of California, Santa Barbara. She has been involved in field and laboratory work in eastern North America, Mexico, and Peru. Her research encompasses a variety of methods, regions, and themes that revolve around the relationship between humans and food in the New World, especially in the periods bracketing the shift to agriculture.

Figure 7.1. Red stone goddess figurine from the Sponemann site, near Cahokia.

The Earth Goddess Cult at Cahokia

Thomas E. Emerson

A scorching, humid, late summer heat, earth baked to concrete, crew members tanned nearly to leather —it was another long, monotonous field season in the American Bottom, the floodplain of the Mississippi River opposite St. Louis, Missouri. Suddenly, something happened on one of those seemingly endless days in 1979 that would hold my professional attention for more than thirty-five years.

My crew and I were digging one of the northernmost archaeological sites along a proposed interstate highway corridor around St. Louis. A light scattering of Mississippian debris littered a small rise in what once was marshland just two miles northeast of Cahokia's Monks Mound. In its modern guise as a cornfield already cut by an interstate highway, the rise was no idyllic setting—the stench of gas and diesel fumes accompanied the deafening roar of interstate traffic. Appropriately, the site bore the name of its car-dealer owner—BBB Motor. My colleagues and I expected little of interest from this modest knoll, but in accordance with federal law, the site had to be investigated.

As we scraped away the plowed earth covering the site, the dig grew more intriguing. Pottery and post holes told us that at about 900 CE, several families of farmers had made their homes on the rise, and by 1050 it had become a special place dedicated to communal mortuary rites. By 1100 it hosted two temples, some free-standing posts and privacy screens, and a small cemetery. Finds of specially engraved pots, medicinal plants, crystals,

and unique, burned deposits of objects, among other things, meant that rituals tied to harvest and life renewal ceremonies had been performed there. Not until late in the excavations, though, did it become clear just how unusual the BBB Motor site really was.

We were following the large earthmover at the edge of the site when a splatter of dusty, brick-red fragments appeared as the machine's blade sliced away another inch of soil. Annoyed, thinking we had cut through historic bricks or tiles, I bent down to pick up a blocky chunk of the stuff. Rolling the piece over in my hand, I became the first person in a thousand years to stare into the face of a Cahokian red stone goddess.

Further excavation in that dusty field revealed the rest of the carving. It was a kneeling woman sinking her stone hoe into the back of a feline-headed serpent lying curled around her knees (plate 14). The serpent's body split into vines sprouting into squash as they swept up her back. The rich symbols of intertwined serpents, agriculture, and women seemed straight out of Mesoamerica and were totally foreign to what we knew about Mississippian art, which often dwelled on men's concerns—war and violence. Later, we found another red stone woman, broken into pieces, in the exposed twelfth-century temple complex. The statuette portrayed a kneeling young woman with a basket at her knees and a plant stalk clutched in her right hand.

Baskets of Ancestors

Earth Mother, bringer of life, is also mistress of the dead. Her baskets and backpack, in Native mythology, are containers for souls and ancestral bones being transported to the land of the living to be reborn. Among the Caddos, Snake Woman carried the first seeds to humans in such containers, often bringing them from the land of the dead. The Skiri Pawnees thought of Lightning, Rain, Dawn, and Night as living in a backpack. Native oral histories indicate that temples often held baskets of bones. Excavations in the Great Mortuary at Spiro Mounds during the 1930s revealed ancestral bones in cane baskets much like the one depicted in this red stone statuette from the BBB Motor site.

Figure 7.2. Cahokian red stone statuette from the BBB Motor site depicting a woman with a basket at her knees and a plant stalk in her right hand.

So spectacular were the finds at BBB Motor that no one dreamed the discovery might be repeated only five years later and less than a mile away. But in 1985, at the Sponemann site, my colleagues Douglas Jackson—a veteran of the BBB Motor excavation—and Andrew Fortier uncovered an even larger temple complex dating between 1100 and 1200 CE. They found the remains of eight pole-and-thatch structures, abundant evidence of ritual events, and hundreds of fragments from at least three female figurines bearing agricultural and fertility motifs.

One thing that made these discoveries so exciting was their rarity. Graven images played little part in the art and iconography of the Native peoples of eastern North America. Their ancient sites, unlike ruins in Mesoamerica, are not strewn with carved stone pillars, engraved friezes, and remnants of stone temples flaunting carvings of gods and goddesses. Even at times when artistic production flourished in the eastern woodlands, such as the Hopewell period, artists seldom depicted human or humanlike ("anthropomorphic") beings or spirits. Mississippian artists occasionally etched or painted such creatures on copper foil, conch shell cups, and ceramic pots, and sometimes they carved them in wood or stone. Yet even at Cahokia, the granddaddy of Mississippian political-religious centers, few excavated mounds and villages have yielded much "art." Unlike at Etowah in Georgia or Spiro in Oklahoma, we have at Cahokia no stacks of copper repoussé plates, no caches of intricately carved shell cups, and few flamboyantly painted or modeled pottery vessels. It is this scarcity of Mississippian portable art that makes Cahokia-style carved red stone figures so stunning.

Early archaeologists had uncovered more than a dozen red stone figures or figurine fragments—mostly depicting men or animals—at Mississippian towns such as Moundville, Shiloh, and Spiro. These isolated specimens were difficult to date, and the source for the red stone was unknown. Because the largest number of them had turned up at Spiro Mounds, scholars initially thought that Caddoan

Figure 7.3. Cahokia-style figurine depicting a chunkey player holding a throwing stone and darts (on left side, not shown).

Southeast. We found that every one was made from flint clay from a single source in Missouri, just west of St. Louis, and Cahokia artisans had carved all of them in the 1100s. These stone figures, we realized, expressed a gendered body of religious, political, and social beliefs intimately linked to Cahokian power and prestige at its height.

But it was not just the recognition that all these artistic masterpieces had been centrally made that revolutionized our thinking about Cahokian religion and art. It was also their subject matter and their contexts. More than a dozen previously known examples from greater Cahokia and the Southeast depict men or animals. One set of Cahokian flint clay figures shows kneeling, naked males, with genitals clearly apparent, often bearing trancelike expressions. The famous sitting male known as the "Resting Warrior," who wears an elaborate cloak and long-nosed-god earplugs (plate 13), falls into this group. Some scholars identify this figure as a mythical character whom the Ho-Chunk people of Wisconsin historically called Red Horn, a culture hero who performed superhuman deeds, including beating giants in a ball game in order to bring his dead father back to life. For Cahokians, I suspect the Resting Warrior more likely represented an elite ancestor who gained power through association with Red Horn's ritual paraphernalia—the human head earplugs, shell bead necklace, and feathered cape.

Among other known male flint clay images, one depicts a player of the Mississippian game of chunkey (chapter 9) holding a throwing stone and darts. Together with the Resting Warrior and several figures of heavily armed and armored warriors in combat, the chunkey player bespeaks elite male preoccupations. Generally, these male figures are found in high-status burials, which suggests that they represented powerful, elite ancestral figures rather than deities.

In unexpected contrast, the half-dozen figures from BBB Motor and the Sponemann site were solely females intertwined with serpents and plant motifs. They seemed to portray an almost stereotypical association of women with agriculture, serpents, fertility, and life renewal. A regional survey of Cahokian figures confirmed that female ones, with

people had carved them in the fourteenth century from a locally available red bauxite. Our discovery of the red stone figures at twelfth-century sites near Cahokia led to the toppling of that theory.

Geological research led by Randall Hughes, a clay mineralogist with the Illinois State Geological Survey, proved that all the carved red stone, from Cahokia to Spiro and Moundville, was a unique form of soft stone called "flint clay." Hughes, Sarah Wisseman, and I collaborated in analyzing all the large red stone figures from Cahokia and across the rare exceptions, were tightly clustered at Cahokia and its surroundings.

What is striking about the female figures is their thematic unity. The premier example of the agricultural theme is the first figurine we found at BBB Motor—the woman wearing a tumpline and pack while hoeing the back of a feline-headed serpent, whose body yields squash vines and fruits. Its counterpart from BBB Motor is the kneeling woman with a basket, her right hand grasping a stalk. The three figurines from the Sponemann site illustrate a similar constellation of traits: women, snakes, baskets, tumplines, stone-bladed hoes, and plant stalks in grasping hands.

Among other examples, a statuette from the Schild site, also just north of Cahokia, depicts a kneeling woman with a possible basket behind her, a pack on her back, a hoe over her shoulder, and a small bag in her hand. An East St. Louis temple contained a carved figure of a kneeling woman holding a shell or gourd cup in her hands. Two female figures found in the Caddo area depict a similar set of motifs. The so-called Woman-at-Mortar figure, made of sandstone but in a Cahokia style, shows a kneeling woman with a woven basket at her knees, a tumpline, a pack on her back, a bag in one hand, and an ear of corn in the other. Yet another Cahokia-style flint clay figure, from Arkansas, reveals a woman kneeling in front of a woven basket, with sunflower and corn stalks growing from her open palms.

These meaning-laden images are so similar that they must represent a common mythical theme. Many researchers believe the woman being portrayed is a female deity whom many Native groups shared in historic times and who is often called Earth Mother. The Earth Mother goddess was conceptually entwined with agricultural and natural fertility, birth, and death; she was the bringer of maize and the mother of humanity. She was intimately tied to the Lower World in Native cosmologies, and in that way she was associated with the moon.

Historically, Native stories about Earth Mother were recorded from Canada to Mesoamerica and from the east coast of North America to the Great Plains. Her names echoed her powers and attributes.

In the Northeast, the Iroquois spoke of Aataentsic, the Grandmother or Old Woman, who brought maize, wore a tumpline and pack, and had lunar associations. The Ojibwas' Nokomis was a moon goddess and mistress of the land of the dead. The Shawnees recognized Our Grandmother, who created all, assisted in childbirth, fashioned the monster-serpent, brought death, provided sacred bundles, and was a lunar goddess.

Looking at a group culturally closer to the Cahokians, the Caddo-speaking peoples of the trans-Mississippi South, we see Native oral histories mesh even more closely with the traits of the Cahokia-style female figures. Historically, these peoples—Pawnee, Caddo, Wichita, and Arikara— had strong ties to Earth Mother and her association with death, the moon, and the evening star. It is among the Caddos that the multifaceted personality of Earth Mother becomes clearest, as exemplified in her string of appellations: Mother Evening Star, Mother Moon, Spider Woman, Mother Corn, Mother Earth, and, strikingly, Snake Woman. In all the goddess's interchangeable facets, Caddos linked her with snakes and death, agricultural abundance, the moon, and the bringing of domesticates and farming skills. For the Caddos, the lunar goddess passed through the stages of life, from young womanhood to old age, with the phases of the moon. The Cahokian goddess images may similarly reflect the lunar passage, for they depict women of different ages. The likelihood that they symbolized the moon seems all the greater since Tim Pauketat's and William Romain's recent recognition of lunar architectural alignments across the Cahokian landscape. The Cahokian Earth Goddess represents one of the clearest associations between a Mississippian deity and historically recorded Native myths.

Cahokian female statuary offers unique insights into Cahokian religion. All examples of known provenience come from discrete religious complexes that contained temples, sacred fire enclosures, mortuary baskets, ritual ceramics, crystals, mica, red cedar, feasting pits, and evidence that people consumed the highly caffeinated "black drink" and used tobacco and hallucinogenic drugs. The BBB Motor and Sponemann sites are archetypal examples of Cahokian temple complexes dedicated to

Figure 7.4. Artist's reconstruction of the great temple atop Monks Mound. In the foreground, a lesser temple or elite building sits on a low pyramid in the Grand Plaza.

fertility, death and life renewal ceremonialism, and Earth Mother. In historic times, French and Spanish explorers reported that Native people in the Southeast used similar temple complexes to store sacred bundles, caches of weapons, ceremonial paraphernalia, ancestral bones in baskets, and discarded objects that contained spiritual power. This spiritual power often required that temple complexes be separated from places of daily activity.

Native temples were fraught with power and danger, and early French and Spanish observers noted that many of them had resident keepers who tended the gods, protected the ritual accouterments, and performed the ceremonies necessary to maintain balance between humans and the cosmos. Often these keepers were tribal elders. At Cahokian temple complexes, archaeologists find everyday cooking and habitation debris, indicating that they, too, had resident keepers. In this case, the keepers

were priests and, very likely, priestesses closely linked to an Earth Mother cult—using cult to mean a religious organization within a society, complete with rules and adherents. This cult, I believe, accompanied the rise of Cahokian central political power. The epitome of sacred places like these might have been a building such as the great temple high atop Monks Mound.

We do not have to simply imagine these priests and priestesses; we have their images frozen in the same red flint clay as the Earth Mother. Statuettes of priestly figures are absent from temples but have been uncovered in graves, where they accompanied their owners to the Lower World. Most of the carvings appear to depict male priests, although I expect female religious practitioners also existed. Just as a Christian minister might wear a cross, so a Cahokian priest, both in real life and carved in stone, carried a gourd rattle. Rattles have long demarked holy and spiritually powerful persons in Native societies, right up the present.

Cahokian priests did many of the things we nowadays associate with shamans—not surprisingly, for they emerged from an earlier, hemisphere-wide, hunter-gatherer shamanistic tradition. Many of the Cahokian red stone figures of priests show them engaging in soul journeys, retaining helper spirits, using religious accouterments, and practicing shape shifting while in an altered state of consciousness. The priest figurines are always drilled to hold a pipe stem, so real-life priests probably used them to smoke trance-inducing tobacco or drugs that helped them engage with the spirit world. Some of the figures' faces appear to show the priest in a narcotic stupor or trance. Others portray him as a shape shifter, transformed into a helper spirit animal such as a bullfrog shaking a rattle in its right hand. Or the stone priest might appear as himself but accompanied by a spirit animal such as a snake, deer, raccoon, or frog.

Regardless of whether the keepers of Cahokia's outlying temple complexes were men, women, or both, I think the city's leaders established these shrines dedicated to an Earth Mother goddess as part of a deliberate strategy. Their goal was to bring order to a sizable rural farming population and gain its loyalty, and farmers might have found rituals honoring the maize-bringing deity especially appealing. In this way the strategy brought into service for the new Cahokian leadership deeply held, pre-Mississippian beliefs about fertility, life renewal, the moon, and the underworld. Those beliefs lived on in descendant Native groups, but Cahokia's fostering of religious complexes devoted to the worship of a specific goddess remains unparalleled in Native eastern North America.

Figure 7.5. Cahokia-style figure of a priest with rattle in right hand and serpent draped around his neck.

Figure 8.1. View from a rise called Little Bluff—site of an early Cahokian religious mission or shrine—across Trempealeau, Wisconsin, and the Mississippi River toward the hills of Minnesota to south.

Early Mississippian Outposts in the North

Robert F. Boszhardt, Danielle M. Benden, and Timothy R. Pauketat

Every summer, canoeists and kayakers depart from the upper reaches of the Mississippi River to journey downstream. Some of them reach St. Louis, about halfway to New Orleans; others make it all the way to the Gulf of Mexico. Occasionally these adventurers write books and blogs about the challenges of their weeks- or months-long trips, commenting on local cuisines, ways of speaking, and other aspects of modern culture along the Mississippi. For fairly obvious reasons, no one paddles up the river—anymore.

Yet nearly a thousand years ago, Mississippian people from the vicinity of Cahokia canoed more than five hundred miles upriver to establish isolated settlements at what are now Stoddard and Trempealeau, Wisconsin. They left Cahokia around 1050 CE—at the dawn of the great city itself—and almost certainly paddled against the current in a flotilla of dugout canoes. Along the way, they had to navigate the Des Moines and Rock Island rapids, each stretching more than ten miles, and pass through lands occupied by other cultural groups. Judging from historical accounts, a canoe voyage from Cahokia to Stoddard and Trempealeau would have taken about thirty days.

At Stoddard, at least some of these migrants established a settlement, and at Trempealeau they built a religious mission or shrine. These early medieval Mississippians brought with them distinctive architectural templates by which to build their houses and mounds, which they laid out in imitation of the celestial geometry used to align buildings and monuments at Cahokia. And they did it all in a territory where people of completely different local cultures already lived.

How do we know this? Why did Mississippians undertake such a journey? What happened to the colonies they established in Wisconsin? Between 2009 and 2011, our team of archaeologists from Illinois and Wisconsin investigated these questions,

Figure 8.2. Locations of Trempealeau, Fisher Mounds, and Aztalan in Wisconsin.

Figure 8.3. Floors of houses built with wall trenches at the Fisher Mounds Site Complex. Each house is about sixteen feet long by eight feet wide.

with support from the National Science Foundation. The story is new and unique for the time period and region, and it begins at a place called the Fisher Mounds Site Complex.

In western Wisconsin, where Coon Creek meets the Mississippi, the modern village of Stoddard sits at the north end of a mile-long peninsula, which for millennia was surrounded by marshes and backwater sloughs. In 1883, anthropologists from the Bureau of American Ethnology visited Stoddard and investigated a string of more than twenty Hopewell burial mounds on the sandy peninsula. In 1929 the Milwaukee Public Museum mapped more of them, all built centuries before the Mississippian era. Archaeologists later dubbed these earthworks the Fisher Mounds Site Complex. Since the 1930s,

when the US government built a lock and dam system along the upper Mississippi that caused wave-induced erosion, residents of Stoddard have found artifacts along the shoreline—among them, interestingly, two Cahokia-style stone disks for playing the game of chunkey (chapter 9) and several stone tools made of chipped chert found near Cahokia.

Still, it was not until 2000, when the US Army Corps of Engineers began sponsoring assessments of the erosion, that archaeologists recognized Mississippian artifacts on the Fisher site peninsula. At the north end of the site complex, they found stone tools made of chert from quarries near Cahokia. They also found pieces of pottery coated with a special red slip (a thin clay coating similar to

Plate 1. Aerial view of the central, or "downtown," Cahokia precinct.

Plate 2. Beakers used to serve the tea known as "black drink" at Cahokia. The designs on the cups represent the ever-moving cosmos and its four winds, or directions.

Plate 3. Artist's rendering of the way Mississippian people might have exchanged stone tools, textiles, pottery, shell, and other goods on the banks of Cahokia Creek, about 1200 CE.

Plate 4. Long-nosed god maskettes made from cut marine shell. Each face is about two inches long.

Plate 5. Carved red stone statuette known as the Keesee figure, showing a Cahokian holding a cylindrical cup in his right hand and kneeling before a pot possibly containing black drink.

Plate 6. Artist's reconstruction of the pyramid-and-causeway complex on Little Bluff at Trempealeau, Wisconsin, viewed from the northeast.

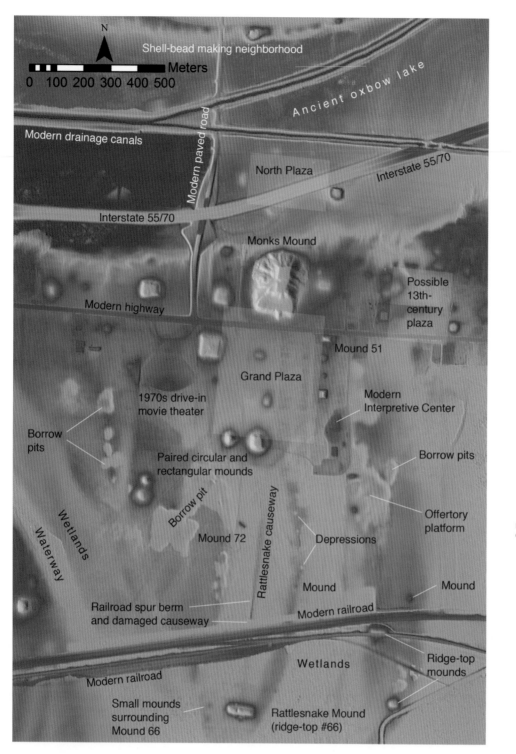

Plate 7. LiDAR view of the north-south axis and earthen pyramids of the central Cahokia precinct.

Plate 8. A Ramey Incised jar from Cahokia decorated with four spiral, or "scroll," motifs and filled with maize kernels.

Plate 9. Carefully crafted chunkey stones from Cahokia. The largest piece is six inches in diameter.

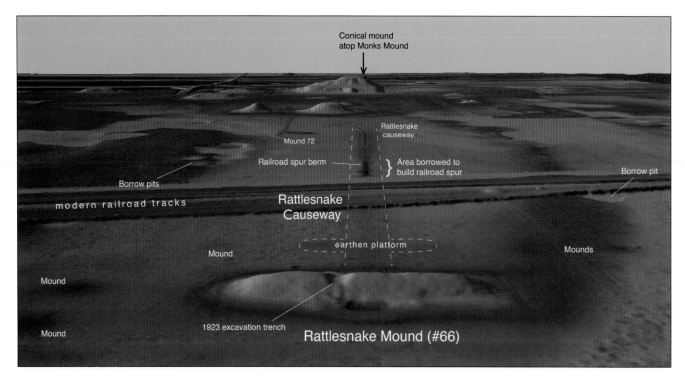

Plate 10. LiDAR image showing the central Cahokia precinct as viewed from the south.

Plate 11. LiDAR image of central Cahokia showing the primary site axis.

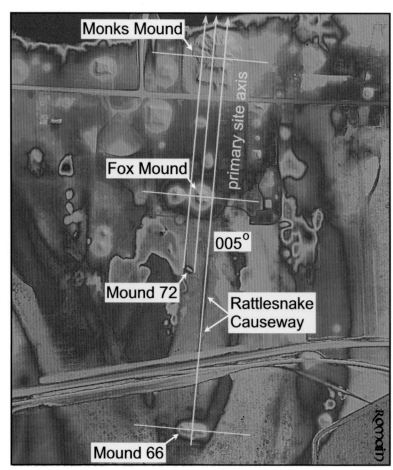

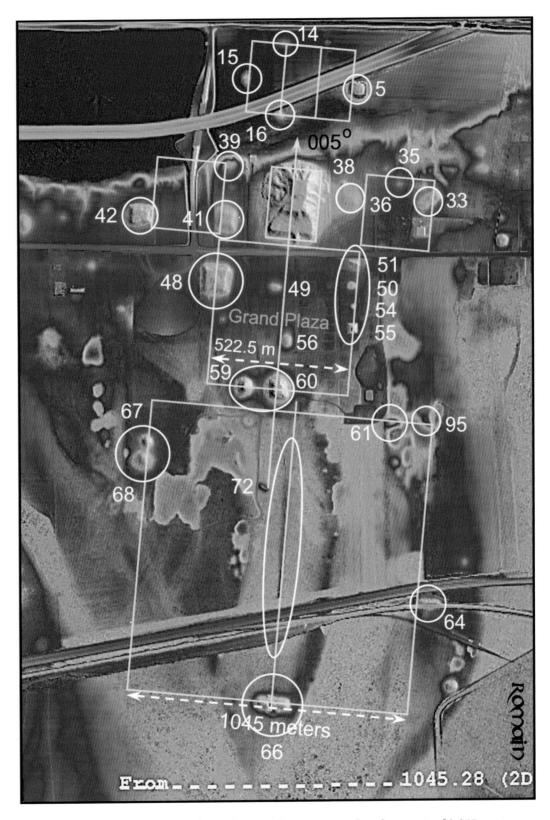

Plate 12. LiDAR image of central Cahokia showing the way squares based on a unit of 1,045 meters were used to lay out the city.

Plate 13. The Cahokian "Resting Warrior" figurine discovered at Spiro Mounds. This prominent man or heroic demigod wears long-nosed-god ear ornaments, a forehead plaque, a shell bead necklace, and a feathered cape. He is sometimes interpreted as the mythical character Red Horn.

Plate 14. Carved red stone statuette from the BBB Motors site depicting a woman with a feline-headed serpent curled around her knees and squash vines sprouting from the serpent's body.

Plate 16. Large Mississippian blades chipped from Dover chert. *Left to right*: oval hoe blade, flared hoe blade, ax head, adze blade (*top*), chisel blade. The largest hoe blade is thirteen inches long.

Plate 15. Large Mississippian blades chipped from Mill Creek chert. *Center*: chisel blade. *Clockwise from top left*: oval hoe blade, notched hoe blade, adze blade, Ramey knife or dagger, flared hoe blade. The largest hoe blade is thirteen inches long.

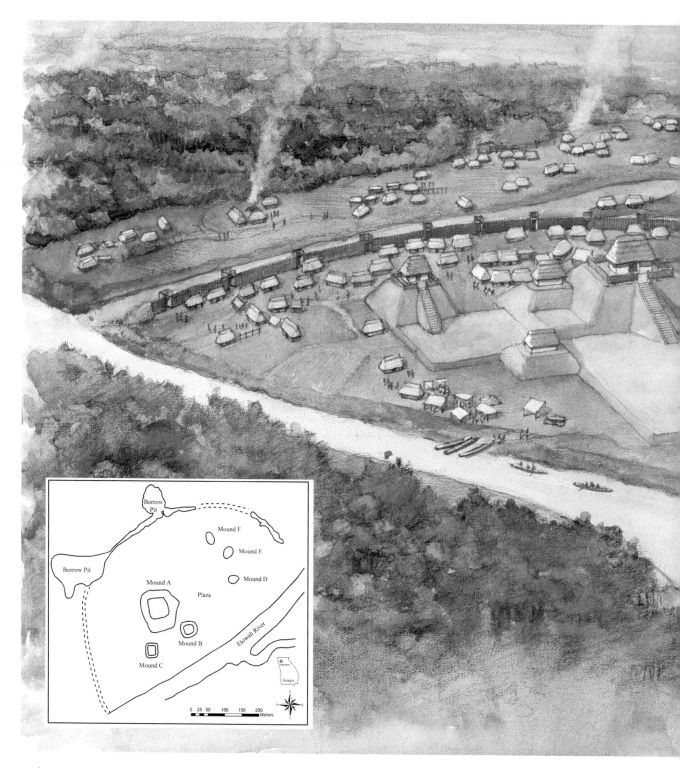

Plate 17. Reconstruction of the Mississippian town of Etowah, in present-day Georgia, at its height in the mid-1300s.

Plate 18. Dyed fabric from Craig Mound at Spiro, Oklahoma. Mississippians spun yarn from plant fibers, rabbit and other animal hair and fur, and feathers from turkeys, geese, and swans. Dyes came from plant roots, flowers, bark, nuts, and a few minerals. The fragment at bottom measures about four inches on a side.

Plate 19. Profile view of excavated Shiloh Mound A, showing colored earth surfaces and sloping pyramid faces.

Plate 20. Computer-generated visualization of the Mississippian town of Upper Nodena, Arkansas, at sunset.

Figure 8.4. Trempealeau Mountain, with the bluffs of Minnesota in the background, on the far side of the Mississippi.

a glaze) and bits of crushed river shells mixed into the clay of the vessel itself—two traits typical of Cahokian dishwares.

In 2009 we set out for Fisher Mounds to excavate a sample of the Mississippian part of the complex. Our dig revealed the remains of four rectangular houses. One of them had single-set post walls, in which each post hole had been dug separately by hand. The other three had wall trenches in the new style developed at Cahokia in the mid-1000s. All the houses were aligned to either cardinal or solstice directions. We also uncovered nearly a thousand imported, Cahokian ceramic and stone artifacts, including fragments of chipped-stone hoe blades. Together these finds told us that although no local people apparently lived in the Coon Creek valley in the 1000s, a colony of Cahokian farmers had moved in around 1050 CE.

Five hundred river miles from Cahokia, the Fisher outpost seems to have occupied a buffer zone between groups of local people of the Effigy Mound culture to the north and south. At Fisher itself, we found no evidence of either trade or conflict between the Mississippians and these effigy mound–building neighbors. The colony was not defensively positioned; its houses were dispersed, not huddled together for protection; and we uncovered few arrowheads. The settlement seems to have been a peaceful colony of Cahokians who brought nearly all their material needs with them, including special pots, stone tools, hoe blades, and chunkey stones. Yet the colony likely existed for only a decade or two, from about 1050 to 1070, and none of the known mounds in the Fisher complex can be attributed to it. Perhaps the Cahokians chose this spot for their small farming colony *because of*

Figure 8.5. The principal earthen pyramid at Aztalan, now a Wisconsin state park. Like Trempealeau, Aztalan was transformed with the influence of Cahokians soon after 1050.

its ancient mounds, as well as its open, uninhabited landscape.

Thirty miles farther upriver, bluffs tower above the Mississippi on both the Wisconsin and Minnesota sides of the river. At the west end of the bluffs on the eastern side is the landmark Trempealeau Mountain, an isolated hill rising from the river's waters. Archaeologically, the point of interest in the area is Little Bluff, a narrow spur at the eastern end of the Trempealeau Bluffs, rising one hundred feet above the modern village of Trempealeau. A remarkable Cahokian outpost once stood on top of Little Bluff, but until our work at the site in 2010 and 2011, researchers knew little about it.

First mapped in 1884, when it was in nearly pristine condition, the Little Bluff site consisted of a modest pyramid-and-causeway complex (plate 6).

The early map shows three connected platform mounds and a causeway. A small ridge-top mound sat on the southernmost platform, at the very tip of Little Bluff. In the early 1900s, Little Bluff property owner and avocational archaeologist George Squier mapped, photographed, and wrote descriptions of the mound complex and the red-slipped pottery he found in his garden below the mounds. He recognized that the platform mounds on Little Bluff resembled those at the better-known Aztalan site in southeastern Wisconsin, the state's premier Mississippian town. There, the mounds once served as foundations for temples or for the residences of religious elites, and Cahokians appear to have lived alongside local Late Woodland people. A palisade wall surrounded Aztalan, which may have come to an end violently around the year 1200.

Figure 8.6. Artifacts from Trempealeau. *Left*: a potsherd of a type called French Fork Incised, typical of the Coles Creek culture. *Right*: Cahokia-style arrowheads. The larger point is 1.25 inches long.

In the 1980s, Wisconsin archaeologists William Green and Roland Rodell discovered more Cahokian pottery along with yet another small platform mound in the middle of the modern village of Trempealeau. They named it the Third Street Mound, a locality within what is now called the Uhl site.

In 2010 and 2011, we came to Trempealeau to learn whether or not this was indeed a Cahokian settlement. Would it be a palisaded town like Aztalan, populated by locals and Cahokians? To find out, we worked on top of Little Bluff and at places in the modern town, including the Uhl site. Our excavations in the Little Bluff pyramid-and-causeway complex turned up scant artifacts and the remains of just one small wall-trench building—good signs that few people had actually lived there. We were excited to discover that the mound complex had been constructed in a single episode. What was more, the builders used distinctively colored soils to cap each layer in the platform mounds—a thick yellow layer topped by a black mantle—just as the builders of greater Cahokia had done, and the Coles Creek people before them. Even a hearth on the floor of the small wall-trench structure on the main mound was covered with a layer of pure yellow silt capped by black fill. Nearby, heavily burned hearths on the mound's surface suggested that people kept fires burning on the Little Bluff summit, as Squier believed had been the case.

Ancient residences lie around the base of Little Bluff. Excavating in three living areas, we found six wall-trench houses, refuse deposits, and scattered fire pits. Many more undoubtedly exist. The excavated rectangular houses were all built using Cahokia's wall-trench construction techniques and might have faced the rising sun at key points in the year. All three areas yielded large quantities of Cahokian pottery and stone tools made from varieties of chert that originated near Cahokia and even as far away as Tennessee (chapter 13). Many of the broken pots were finely made bowls and jars in which people may have once served special meals and ritual medicines. One vessel, of a type called French Fork Incised, was made by someone associated with the Coles Creek culture. The stone tools included many knives imported from Cahokia and several finely made, Cahokia-style projectile points. A half dozen of these points, all thin and well made, lay scattered across the floor of one abandoned house, where we think they were left as offerings. Glossy stone flakes discarded when residents resharpened hoes suggest that these people, too, were farmers.

Our archaeological finds confirm that some of the earliest Mississippians left the burgeoning city of Cahokia, paddled more than five hundred miles upriver, and settled at Stoddard and then Trempealeau, building houses and an impressive bluff-top mound complex according to Cahokian architectural conventions. What motivated them to do so? Did they depart their homeland voluntarily or under duress? Had they any prior knowledge of their destination? Did they hope to extend

Cahokia's economic base or perhaps to proselytize foreign peoples to a new religion?

We think the settlers left home voluntarily. The predominance of stone and pottery from Cahokia among their possessions suggests that some colonists felt free to return to the homeland periodically to replenish their stock. Once in the north, the Cahokians lived in scattered, unprotected dwellings; they clearly perceived no threat from locals. They seem to have felt right at home in Wisconsin.

We also think the Cahokian migrants knew about their destination before leaving, because so far no early Mississippian settlements are known to have existed between Cahokia and Wisconsin that might have served as way stations during the long trek north. It looks as if the colonists headed straight for Stoddard and Trempealeau. Perhaps they had heard of the territory now called the Driftless Area, which covers all of southwestern Wisconsin and portions of adjacent Illinois, Iowa, and Minnesota. Never scoured by glaciers, the Driftless Area is a topographic island—a rugged, forested landscape known for its rock shelters and craggy springs, abounding in wild plant and animal foods—in a sea of glaciated terrain. Exactly how the Cahokians learned about the Driftless Area remains unknown. It is plausible that Effigy Mound people visited Cahokia, bringing glowing descriptions of their homeland, or that Cahokian scouts explored the upper Mississippi in advance of the long journey to Stoddard. But so far we have no archaeological evidence for either scenario.

Some archaeologists assume that Mississippians established colonies like those at Stoddard and Trempealeau for economic reasons—to acquire goods or materials unavailable close to home. Yet almost no evidence exists that the Fisher Mounds and Trempealeau settlers were shipping resources back to Cahokia. Excavations in central Cahokia have turned up a few arrowheads made from a sparkling, hardened sandstone mined in Wisconsin, and in the East St. Louis precinct artisans used small amounts of a soft, purple Wisconsin pipestone for making earspools. These artifacts are so rare, though, that exporting their raw materials from a place like Trempealeau cannot have been big business. Another possible export from the north

was wild rice, but no wild rice grains have been found at Cahokia.

We think it possible that rather than being an economic colony, the Trempealeau outpost—and perhaps in some way even the Fisher Mounds locality—served as a Cahokian religious mission. Set in the scenic and mysterious Driftless Area, Trempealeau's bluff-top pyramid complex and at least one other mound offer ample evidence of transplanted Cahokian beliefs and ceremonies. Even the refuse in Trempealeau's habitation areas includes large proportions of ritual pottery and special stone tools. We think it likely that Cahokians made the arduous journey upriver to experience the unusual northern world and practice their religion within the surrounding territory occupied by Late Woodland, Effigy Mound people.

Whether or not they succeeded is another question. The Mississippian presence, with its colorful platform mounds, distinctive architecture, elaborate rituals, exotic stone, and red pots, might have overwhelmed the indigenous people, but there is scant evidence that the two groups interacted with each other directly. Perhaps the locals mingled with Cahokians for religious outings and mound building while remaining separate in their daily lives. Or perhaps they simply never embraced the ways of the interlopers in their midst.

Whatever the case, the Stoddard and Trempealeau colonies both proved short-lived, surviving for only a decade or two before being abandoned. We do not know whether they failed or, perhaps, succeeded as intentionally short-term outreach projects by Cahokians who achieved their goals in the north and then moved on. Maybe these southern Mississippians lacked the resources to sustain themselves for the long haul, or maybe a leader perished and the Trempealeau mission suddenly folded. At this point, we can only speculate.

For several decades after the colonies' abandonment, there seems to have been no Mississippian presence in the northern hinterlands. Then, around 1100 CE—a generation after the Stoddard and Trempealeau colonies—Cahokian pots, other objects, and iconography appeared in the north again, this time reaching from northwestern Iowa all the way to Lake Michigan. Archaeologically, this surge of things and styles is marked by the widespread appearance of Cahokian-manufactured Ramey Incised pottery and its imitations made in the north. At this later time, many northern sites show material hints of contact with Cahokians far to the south. But researchers have discovered no later sites like those at Stoddard and Trempealeau, sites that clearly were missions populated entirely by southerners. Times after 1100 were no longer entirely peaceful, either. Several sites with Ramey pottery, including Aztalan, were fortified, and excavators have found evidence in human skeletons for traumatic injury and death.

By 1150, the now Mississippianized peoples of the northern Midwest began to regroup in northwestern Illinois and eastern Minnesota. Expansive villages became the norm, marking the beginning of what archaeologists call the "Oneota" culture. True to their Mississippian heritage, most of the designs on early Oneota cooking pots look like spinoffs of Ramey Incised designs, suggesting that Cahokian inspirations were now less direct and fading. The new Oneota identities flourished across the northern Midwest until Europeans arrived.

Robert F. Boszhardt has worked in the upper Mississippi Valley since 1980, with an emphasis on the unglaciated Driftless Area. Although he specializes in ceramic and lithic analyses, his research has touched on nearly all aspects of the region's archaeology. He is the author of *Deep Cave Rock Art in the Upper Mississippi Valley* (2003) and co-author of *Twelve Millennia: Archaeology of the Upper Mississippi River Valley* (2003).

Danielle M. Benden is senior curator in the Department of Anthropology at the University of Wisconsin–Madison. Her curatorial interests focus on rehabilitating museum collections for research and on training next-generation archaeologists. Her field research focuses on the early presence of Mississippian peoples at sites in the Upper Mississippi River Valley.

Figure 9.1. Competitors playing the game of chunkey in a medieval Mississippian town.

The Game of Chunkey

Thomas J. Zych

All across eastern North America in the last few centuries before Europeans arrived—and even long afterward—Native people played a game of skill and endurance called chunkey. But like most other sporting events, chunkey was more than a simple game. Just as our modern Olympics unite nations and allow people of different backgrounds to share in a common experience, so chunkey helped to unite medieval Mississippian players and spectators alike.

Researchers believe chunkey started several hundred years before the rise of Cahokia as a children's game played around the home. When Mississippian lifestyles spread outward from the city-center of Cahokia in the 1000s and early 1100s CE, chunkey became transformed into a grand public event, a new way for assorted peoples to coalesce under a common identity.

Today, circular stone discs, usually two to five inches in diameter, are virtually the only evidence we have of this once cherished pastime. Much of what we know about the rules of ancient chunkey comes from the written accounts of early Euro-american travelers, who watched American Indians playing the game into the twentieth century. Although chroniclers' accounts vary, people played chunkey much the same way everywhere.

At the start of play, two contestants stood side by side at the edge of a field, facing an upright wooden post off in the distance. Each man held a long wooden pole or staff. One player hurled a chunkey stone on its edge across the length of the field toward the post. As soon as he released the stone, both players ran forward and launched their poles after the rolling disc. The objective was for a player to make his pole hit the moving chunkey stone or land closest to its center once it stopped (the precise rules varied from place to place). The player who did so scored points for that round. Often, the poles featured notches or tassels, and scoring could depend on which notch or tassel touched or almost touched the stone. Play continued until one contestant reached a predetermined score and was declared the winner.

Historically, chunkey matches could last all day, the players running relentlessly back and forth across the field. The game undoubtedly demanded great skill and stamina. Among the historic Muskogee, Cherokee, and Choctaw nations, men played chunkey on large, rectangular plots of ground called "chunk-yards," each marked by a large post standing in its center. Chunk-yards often lay in the center of the town, near the community's public or ceremonial buildings. Playing surfaces were leveled, smoothed, covered with fine sand, and swept daily. Large crowds of spectators, including people from neighboring towns and farming settlements, gathered to watch the matches and to root for—and gamble on—their favorite players.

Figure 9.2. A chunk-yard as it might have appeared in a Mississippian town.

Archaeological evidence of the chunkey game first appears in deposits dating to the 600s CE along the Mississippi River in western Illinois and eastern Missouri. Early chunkey stones were typically tiny, only an inch or two in diameter, and crudely made of fire-hardened clay or rough stone. Perhaps they were fashioned by the same children and young adults who played the game. By 900 CE, chunkey stones appear more frequently in the archaeological record and are usually larger and more carefully crafted than their predecessors.

One hundred and fifty years later, the first Cahokians turned this local game into a public, perhaps city-wide event and carried it with them as they lengthened their reach up and down the Mississippi Valley. When excavating Mississippian sites, archaeologists often find chunkey stones near open plazas or adjacent to public buildings, which suggests that the game had become more than just household recreation. Cahokian artisans began finely handcrafting chunkey discs from choice kinds of raw stone. Ground to a more or less standard shape and size, these discs had two concave sides (plate 9). The style spread quickly as the Cahokians introduced their version of the chunkey game to the hinterlands.

To the north, Cahokians brought the sport with them to Fisher Mounds, Trempealeau, and Aztalan in south-west and south-central Wisconsin. Cahokian-style chunkey stones have been found at all these sites. Meanwhile, stones also began to appear throughout the southwestern Great Lakes region. Game discs made there were similar in size to Cahokia-style stones but often thicker and heavier. Some such hinterland stones, like Cahokia's well-made varieties, had holes in their middles.

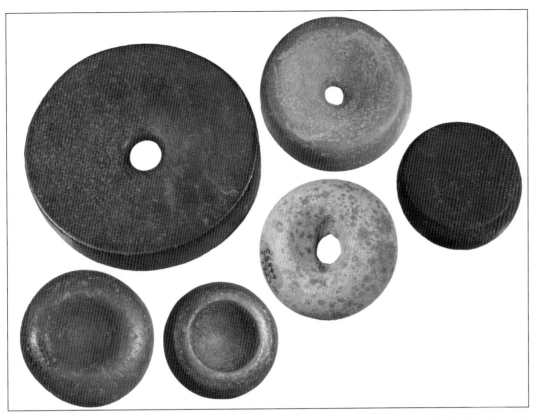

Figure 9.3. Chunkey stones from the western Great Lakes. The largest piece is five and a half inches in diameter.

After 1050, chunkey spread into the southeastern part of the continent. At the early Mississippian mound site of Shiloh in southwestern Tennessee, excavators found chunkey stones buried on and below the platform mounds. By the time Cahokia attained its peak population in the 1100s, the game had reached towns as far away as Angel, in Indiana; Kincaid, in Illinois; and Ocmulgee and Etowah, in Georgia.

As the popular pastime became part of a shared notion of community or even of ethnic identity, particular stones likely came to be associated with specific families, lineages, or even whole towns. For example, excavation at Mound 72, a burial mound at Cahokia, revealed fifteen chunkey stones buried alongside offerings of rolled sheet copper (possibly a copper-covered staff or rod), sheets of mica (a mirrorlike crystal from North Carolina), and large caches of stone-tipped arrows. The chunkey stones and other valued objects might have been associated with particular social groups who placed them in the mound as offerings.

Chunkey long outlived the Cahokians. But as the sport literally and figuratively rolled across the landscape, it gave Mississippianized people new opportunities to meet, share in a common worldview, and create mutual histories. It might also have given rival groups a relatively peaceful means of resolving conflicts. Hugely popular, chunkey helped knit Native peoples together all across the medieval Mississippian world.

Thomas J. Zych is a part time instructor in the Department of Sociology and Anthropology at the University of Toledo. His research interests include Late Woodland-Middle Mississippian community contact during the eleventh and twelfth centuries, with a special focus on the Aztalan site in southeastern Wisconsin.

Figure 10.1. *The King and Queen of the Timucua*, northern Florida, engraving made by Theodor de Bry after a 1564 painting by Jacques Le Moyne. "Sometimes in the evening the king goes for a walk with his first wife. He wears a stag skin, elegantly prepared and painted.... The queen and her handmaidens wear a kind of moss...woven into delicate tresses that make chains of an azure blue.... All of the chiefs and their wives have their bodies tattooed."

The Fabric of Mississippian Society

Susan M. Alt

While excavating at the Grossmann site, a small Mississippian administrative complex in the hills east of Cahokia, my crew and I had one of those singular moments of awe and joy when we realized that the shards of a stonelike material being found in a pit were actually pieces of a heat-exploded, carved, red stone smoking pipe. It had been fashioned in the shape of an owl. While carefully uncovering the pipe fragments, we were even more surprised when we recognized that the charred debris surrounding them also contained bits of carbonized woven fabric with burned seeds and corn kernels clinging to them. It was difficult to say which item was rarer, the fabric or the stone pipe!

These finds startled us because we never expected to find intact fabric in a pit at a Mississippian site. Fabric is perishable; it seldom lasts long in acidic midwestern and southeastern soils, and certainly not for nearly a thousand years. Even if it survived the soil, humid air and changeable weather stood ready to hasten disintegration. The same problems hold true for the discovery of cordage, matting, and basketry in archaeological sites. But sometimes, when just the right conditions exist, one finds the unexpected.

As it turned out, the fabric was not alone. We uncovered the charred outlines of a woven bag in another pit full of burned debris—more

Figure 10.2. Excavation of a charred net bag in a pit at the Grossmann site, Richland complex, east of Cahokia, 2002.

heat-exploded bits of stone tools and pottery. These ash-laden deposits had all been burned in or intentionally placed in the pits and then capped with a clayey soil, sealed away for centuries. The alkaline-rich ash neutralized the naturally acidic soil, the clayey cap lent some protection from weathering, and that which normally decays came to be preserved.

We now believe this burying of burned objects in pits was a part of ritual or ceremonial events at the Grossmann site. The fragments of fabric seem to have been the remains of bags or wrappings that held corn, seeds, and other items significant in the lives of the people who burned them. They might also have been parts of medicine bundles—wrapped collections of sacred objects—that were burned in the pits. People must have gathered certain items, prayed over them, and then thrown them into the fire as part of a celebration such as a renewal cere-mony—something like the historically known Green Corn celebration, in which participants destroyed old possessions and created new ones.

Figure 10.3. The charred bag at the bottom of the pit.

We have since found evidence of similar kinds of events elsewhere in the greater Cahokia region, such as an elaborate burning cere-mony in a decommissioned temple at the Emerald site, fifteen miles east of Cahokia. There, baskets filled with materials now unrecognizable were piled up and incinerated as part of the ritual closure of the temple. The Mississippian period saw more elaborate public rituals than the preceding Late Woodland period did, as well as greater differentia-tion between people by status and occupation. People all over the world have long used textiles and fabric to make statements about who they are, what they do, and what status they can claim. Textiles can be valuable goods that are traded, gifted, displayed, and even sacrificed, as they seemingly were at the Grossmann site.

To create fabric, someone first had to turn fibers

into thread or yarn that could be woven, braided, or twined. In the Mississippian world, people made yarns of plant fibers such as dogbane, milkweed, and nettle, along with animal fibers such as dog and rabbit hair. Some yarns also contained feathers or down from turkeys, geese, and other birds. From these raw materials, a person could produce yarns as coarse as rope or as fine as the softest linens. Creating yarn required that the chosen material be collected at the appropriate time, worked into fine, thin strips, softened, and then twisted into a thread.

Often the maker spun the raw fibers together into a single cord simply by rolling them along the thigh. (Native North Americans did not use spin-ning wheels.) In another method, the spinner attached fibers to one end of a smooth stick, or spindle, which she held vertically and set spinning.

Figure 10.4. Spindle whorls fashioned from pieces of broken pottery, from the Halliday site, Richland complex, east of Cahokia. The largest whorl is about six inches in diameter.

The spindle stayed in motion through the action of a counterweight or flywheel—a circular disk known as a spindle whorl—fastened to the bottom of the spindle. The spinner drew the raw fibers out of their bundle with her fingers, and the spindle's motion twisted them into yarn or cordage.

In the Midwest and Southeast, people usually made spindle whorls from recycled pieces of broken pots. They chipped each potsherd into a circle and then drilled a hole through it to accept the spindle. In the hands of an experienced spinner, a spindle with a whorl produced more thread, yarn, or cordage much more quickly than could be done without one. A spindle and whorl also permitted less-skilled spinners to manufacture large amounts of cordage.

Spindle whorls in archaeological sites around greater Cahokia tell us that the early Mississippians spun yarn—and presumably wove cloth—in abundance. Excavators find the largest numbers of spindle whorls in deposits dating to the first hundred years of Cahokia's history, between 1050 and 1150, so we infer that the earliest Cahokians, with their burgeoning population and expanding power, had great need of fabric. And the whorls are more concentrated in the refuse of some families, in some

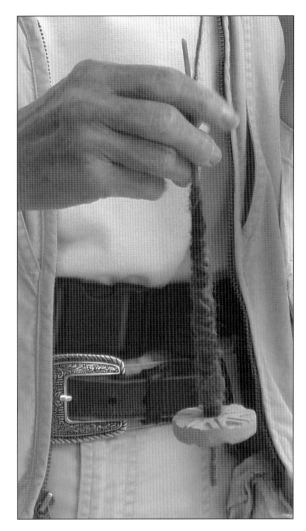

Figure 10.5. Use of the spindle and spindle whorl.

neighborhoods or villages, than in the refuse of others. The very greatest known density of spindle whorls is at the Halliday site, which we believe was a farming village where immigrants to the Cahokia region lived. Such concentrations of spindle whorls suggest that some villages, or a few people in certain villages, specialized in producing textiles to fill Cahokia's demand for more cloth more quickly than ever before. At Halliday and similar sites, farmers lived exceedingly modest lives devoted mostly, we think, to growing surplus crops and weaving fabric for use at Cahokia.

Textiles might have gained importance in Mississippian times because people were becoming more differentiated into statuses such as common farmer, elite priest or administrator, and skilled artisan. Just like people today, Mississippians signaled their identity, social status, occupation, and other attributes through the fabrics, colors, and types of garments and ornaments they wore. For example, the bodies of important people buried in mounds were wrapped in cloth that might be studded with shell beads or woven to show a design. In fragments of fabric uncovered at Craig Mound, part of the Spiro site in Oklahoma, turkey, goose, and swan feathers had been woven into the material. Fabrics found with elite burials in ridge-top mounds often show relatively complex weaving techniques, unusual raw materials such as rabbit fur and bird down, and fine threads closely woven or twined together. Traces of textiles observed in another way, as imprints on pottery surfaces, sometimes display coarser fibers. Some fragments of cloth have been found that look like fine linen, and indeed, dogbane, a plant Mississippians often spun into yarn, is a relative of the European flax plant used to create linen.

Figure 10.6. A fragment of twined tapestry depicting a human face, from Craig Mound at Spiro, Oklahoma. The yarns were dyed before being woven.

Evidence from burials and from art on shells and carved pipes tells us that high-status persons wore elaborate garments. One woman buried at the Aztalan site, in Wisconsin, went to her grave wearing clothing—possibly sashes—sewn with bands of marine shell beads. At least two important Cahokians were laid to rest wearing capes onto which had been sewn thousands of shells from sea snails of the genus Marginella and disk beads cut from the shells of conchs. Just such a Cahokian character seems to be depicted in a carved flint-clay figure later buried at Spiro Mounds. This red stone carving, known as the Resting Warrior (plate 13), portrays an important man seated and wearing a headdress, long-nosed-god earpieces, a shell bead necklace, and a cape covered in feathers. From other images in Mississippian art, we can surmise that the clothing of elites included skirts, breechcloths, capes, belts, sashes, headgear, and footwear. Many garments were dyed in vibrant colors (plate 18). Studies have suggested that to wear garments colored red or featuring fringed edges, a person had to be an elite. Mississippian art also shows that everyday clothing may have been just a skirt for women and a breechcloth for men.

Mounds like Craig at Spiro have given researchers some of the best-preserved pieces of Mississippian fabric, because of the way the mounds were built. Each addition to the mound was capped with a heavy layer of clay, which created an unusual environment that sealed and protected what was inside the mound. Excavators

Figure 10.7. Disk beads from Cahokia like those sewn onto special capes and burial shrouds. These beads were made from conch shells imported from the Gulf of Mexico.

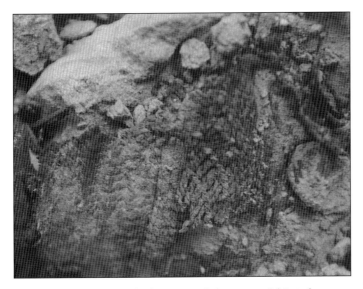

Figure 10.8. Close-up of a fragment of plain twined fabric from Kunnemann Mound, Cahokia.

have discovered textiles not only in Craig Mound but also in Mounds R and W at Moundville, Alabama; Mound C at Etowah; Mound A at Shiloh; and the Wilson and Kunnemann mounds at Cahokia.

Textiles from all these places demonstrate the skill and artistry of Mississippian spinners and weavers. Even the relatively few samples of Mississippian textiles we have represent a variety of styles for weaving, plaiting, and twining, so it seems clear that textile production was a complex and diverse industry. Weavers achieved different styles of textiles with different designs by varying the mechanics of twining or weaving and by incorporating elements in different textures. They colored cloth by intermixing fibers of different natural colors and by using dyes and paints.

Because archaeologists recover perishable goods so rarely, we tend to underappreciate the importance of fabric and garments in the daily lives of ancient people, as well as in maintaining social and political boundaries. Some researchers have estimated that as much as 90 percent of the material goods in Mississippian households was perishable, and textiles made up a large portion of that total. People in the past spent a great deal of time collecting raw materials, preparing fibers from them, finding substances such as madder roots and walnuts to boil into dyes, spinning yarns, and then assembling them into cloth, baskets, mats, shoes, and many other necessary, day-to-day objects. Ignoring these industries denies not only the social value of perishable items but also much of the labor put into daily living.

Any image we have of people living in a Mississippian city or town should show them wearing cloth skirts and twined shoes, sometimes accompanied by capes, head wraps, and sashes. Their capes often were complex fabrics, woven with multiple patterns and stitches, dyed or painted red, yellow, black, and brown. Fringes on some capes would have emphasized movement, swirling when worn during dances. Elaborately carved fasteners held garments together, and hairpins kept coiffures in place. Woven mats and painted cloths decorated the walls and covered the floors of people's wooden houses. Altogether, glimpses of the Mississippians' textile arts let us see how their skills brought beauty into their daily lives. Images of people wearing deerskins and living in skin tents simply do not apply to the medieval Mississippians.

Figure 11.1. Earthen pyramids at the Angel site, a large Mississippian town on the lower Ohio River.

Lost Mississippian Towns Found on the Ohio

Staffan Peterson

The social lives and histories of the many tens of thousands of medieval Mississippians in the American Midwest and South might seem lost to us today, difficult to find, much less understand. But the stunning arrays of preserved platform mounds at places like Cahokia beckon us to try. I have looked for traces of the lives and histories of Mississippian peoples at the ancient towns of Angel and Kincaid, both on the banks of the lower Ohio River—Kincaid in the Black Bottom of extreme southeastern Illinois and Angel farther up the Ohio in southwestern Indiana (map 3). The two towns were among the largest in the Mississippian world. Both were historically connected to Cahokia, and their distinctive pyramidal mounds are our first clues to their common Mississippian history.

Of course the mounds speak to only a part of medieval American history. How can we understand the rest? Just beneath the surface lies much more evidence—the preserved footprints of houses, temples, storehouses, public plazas, great palisade walls, gardens, open fields, workshops, and walkways. New technologies are making it possible to learn more about what made such Mississippian towns Mississippian.

Angel was the central place of a Mississippian group living along a forty-mile stretch of the Ohio River from about 1100 to 1400 CE. It was the closest major center by land to Cahokia, some 135 miles to the west-northwest. At one time, a timber

and daub palisade enclosed about ninety-two acres at Angel. That palisaded area is now a national historic landmark and an Indiana state historic site.

Kincaid was the center of another province, this one even larger. Its history and layout paralleled Angel's, although its palisaded area covered at least 128 acres. Situated near modern-day Metropolis, Illinois, the ruins of Kincaid occupy a wide floodplain eighty-two miles downriver from Angel as the crow flies. Recently I participated in high-tech surveys of both towns using a method called magnetometry to map what lies below their surfaces. The results are altering the means by which we understand the medieval Mississippians, enabling us to "see" the traces of these towns without digging.

In the 1920s and 1930s, the large groups of mounds along the Mississippi and Ohio Rivers and their tributaries became tempting targets for the emerging profession of scientific archaeology. On the Ohio River, at the southernmost tip of Illinois, the University of Chicago began to study Kincaid. The Indiana Historical Society and avocational archaeologists began to explore Angel. Both sites were obviously something extraordinary, yet what kinds of places they were, who created them, and when they flourished were completely unknown. Had they been ceremonial centers, villages, or something else? Were they somehow related to each other or to towns in other regions that looked similar? How many people lived in each place? When

Figure 11.2. Earthen pyramids at the Kincaid site.

was each abandoned, and why? Answers to even such basic questions require huge quantities of data, and the very sizes of Mississippian towns make accumulating such data a challenge.

At Kincaid and Angel, excavation campaigns that began in those early years and have continued into the present did produce vast quantities of artifacts and information. With those data, researchers can at last start to address vexing questions about the two places. That both embraced a similar culture seems clear. Great similarities exist between pottery styles, domestic and civic architecture, and decorative motifs at Kincaid, Angel, and some other large Mississippian towns. Although the sizes and shapes of many of the mounds vary, both Kincaid and Angel feature large, flat-topped earthen pyramids, now understood to be classic Mississippian architecture. At both sites, archaeologists also find low, circular mounds, evidence of enclosing palisades with defensive bastions or perhaps guard towers, and, below ground, the remains of hundreds of Mississippian-style wall-trench houses. These discoveries prove that these places were not purely ceremonial centers but also were thriving towns.

Archaeologists have always known that the shovel-and-trowel approach is a difficult way to understand large sites. It is slow, expensive, and sometimes short on the kind of information needed.

At Angel, for example, even after more than twenty-five seasons of excavations, the total area dug is about four acres, or just over 4 percent of the whole palisaded area. The situation is similar at Kincaid. Since the importance of these places lies partly in their great size, it is hard to understand them from small excavated samples.

Excavation is destructive, too. Archaeologists nowadays try to do as little of it as possible, especially at protected sites like Angel, Kincaid, and Cahokia. For decades, researchers have been looking for ways to assess large areas without destroying the evidence. Fortunately for archaeology, in the 1950s, scientists interested in underground mapping for mining exploration began to experiment with methods of using natural properties of the earth itself to see beneath the surface.

The best known of these methods relies on the earth's magnetism. The needle of a compass is driven by a magnetic field created by iron present in the planet's core as well as in bedrock and soil. Naturally occurring iron in the soils of archaeological features emits a magnetic signal far weaker than that of the earth's core, but still measureable. When soil is disturbed, as happens when people build, its natural magnetic profile becomes disturbed, too. Iron oxides in soil where houses once stood, in fired clay daub, and in earthen monuments—all of which abound at Kincaid and Angel—create strong

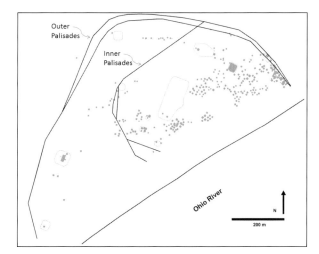

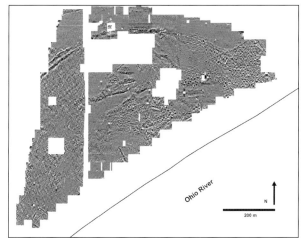

Figure 11.3. Schematic map of the Angel site (*top*), derived largely from a magnetometer image of same area (*bottom*).

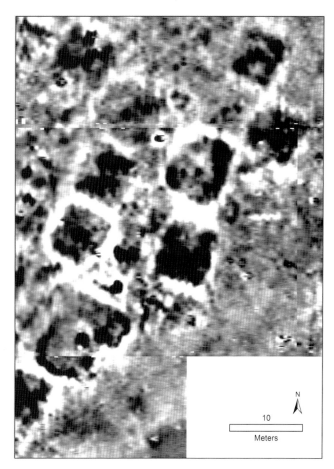

Figure 11.4. Closeup of the magnetometer map for Angel, showing the footprints of a cluster of aligned, pole-and-thatch buildings whose floors lay slightly below the original ground surface.

magnetic contrasts between archaeological features and their surroundings. As a result, magnetometry surveys at the two sites yield large-scale, maplike images of entire sites or neighborhoods, comparable to aerial photographs. The images tell us much in themselves and also reveal promising targets for later excavation, which, destructive or not, will always be crucial in archaeology. Only by digging can we firmly identify what we see in magnetic maps, uncover artifacts that can be dated, and obtain detailed information about building techniques, craft production, foodways, and more.

Magnetic survey results can be challenging to interpret, partly because they reveal a palimpsest of all the activity that ever happened at a given place. For Angel and Kincaid, though, our results were good enough that we could detect buried features

including houses, plazas, mounds, and palisades, all seen for the first time in six or seven centuries. The new maps told us that ninety years after the start of excavations at the two towns, we researchers still had known little about where things were.

Now, studying the magnetic survey images, we can see hundreds of otherwise invisible Mississippian houses. Geophysical instruments detect them readily because of their relatively large floor areas, rectangular shapes, partly below-ground construction, fired clay hearths, wall trenches, and daub walls. At Angel, the footprints of about 250 houses show up in the magnetic maps, although those footprints probably represent many more individual houses rebuilt in the same places. Excavations uncovered an additional 94 houses, bringing the number of structures at Angel—not counting rebuildings—to nearly 350, built and used over the town's three-hundred-year life span. The survey also showed that houses there varied little in size and shape. Nearly all of them were square, with an average floor area of a little more than four hundred square feet.

At Kincaid we surveyed only about half the town magnetically, but we estimate that we found nearly eight hundred structure footprints. Again, many of them represent houses rebuilt on top of one another, so the total house count over the life of the town—some three centuries—could well be more than two thousand. As at Angel, almost all buildings at Kincaid were square or nearly square, but house size seems to have varied depending on location in the town. For instance, houses in one group associated with a low mound or house platform measure less than half the average Kincaid house size, whereas those associated with a plaza are slightly larger than average. Excavation data show that the smaller houses were built earlier in the town's history than the larger ones. This may mean that, as is also known at Cahokia, households grew larger later in time, with each roof covering extended families and providing for more storage space.

Towns everywhere usually have districts, precincts, or neighborhoods in which people interact face-to-face. At both Angel and Kincaid, our magnetic maps show that houses typically stood clustered together, most of them within a few yards of each other. Rows of houses with what look like pathways between them can be detected. Two house clusters at Angel each consisted of at least six structures in three rows, and we see similar patterns at Kincaid. Excavation data augment the maps by showing that residents often rebuilt houses at the same angles as previous buildings and on the same house lots. This suggests some continuity of ownership, perhaps through inheritance. It is difficult to determine archaeologically whether the house clusters constitute what we think of as neighborhoods, but certainly it appears that the towns' social organization rested at least partly on multihousehold groups.

Typically in Mississippian towns, such groups lived clustered around a community plaza. Kincaid

Figure 11.5. Computer-generated, three-dimensional map of house locations near Angel's Mound A.

and Angel each boasted a large public square. At Kincaid, magnetometry showed that the area thought to be the plaza was indeed largely free of buildings, as one would expect. At Angel, an early investigator had inferred a plaza location, and our magnetic study did detect a large, level, open area southeast of the largest platform mound, Mound A. Subsequent excavations in this open area revealed that the normal soil profile had been altered, meaning that the plaza itself was a constructed feature. Built by leveling the natural, undulating landform through cut-and-fill operations, Angel's plaza—like similar ones at Cahokia and other Mississippian towns—demanded an enormous amount of labor in its construction. If, as seems likely, the plaza was built at the same time as Mound A, then I think the early center of the town was planned, and a large force of workers executed that plan.

Considerable labor was also devoted to building the palisade walls at Angel and Kincaid. Similarly large palisades are known from downtown Cahokia and most other Mississippian towns across the Midwest and South for at least part of each town's history. These wooden walls were likely defensive, but against whom the residents of Angel and Kincaid had to defend themselves is a mystery. Could they have been at war with each other? Or might the wall have been built at the founding of each town in order to forestall warring, not unlike

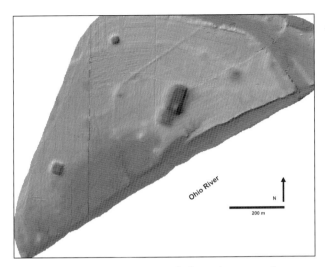

Figure 11.6. Computer-generated, three-dimensional map of the Angel site showing the long, semicircular remains of daubed wooden palisade walls.

the arms races of the modern era? The latter seems possible, because there is no clear sign that any all-out assault took place at either town.

Understanding when the palisades were built and where they stood in relation to mounds and houses can be key in understanding the original purpose of the palisade constructions and the seriousness of the military threat. Until our magnetometry survey, detailed information about the location and timing of palisade construction had eluded archaeologists. At Kincaid, the survey detected a palisade far outside what had previously been believed to be the outermost wall. This new palisade increased the enclosed area of the town by more than twenty-five acres. It suggests that war or the threat of war was an ongoing possibility for this growing community.

At Angel, researchers had long suspected that three major episodes of palisade construction took place, but their locations and timing were not entirely understood. The magnetic survey identified the locations of all three. Excavations guided by our new map then enabled us to obtain material associated with each palisade for radiocarbon dating. Contrary to expectations, the palisade enclosing the largest area turned out to have been built first, suggesting that the town was founded all at once, with a clear plan in mind, rather than growing slowly over time. The existence of an encircling

wall from the town's very beginning, augmented by two later walls inside the first, suggests that—as at Kincaid—the threat of attack existed throughout the town's history.

One surprising result of our studies was that about 80 percent of the space inside the largest palisade at Angel contained no architecture. At Kincaid, the situation was the reverse: nearly 80 percent of the space had been built upon. In both places, however, the density of houses in their respective neighborhoods proved to be about the same—a little under three houses per acre. Both towns seem to have enclosed approximately four times more space than residents actually lived on. We do not yet know what they used all that space for, but I expect future study will show the presence of gardens or fields. If townspeople felt themselves under threat of attack, they might have wanted at least some of their fields inside the palisade for protection while at work farming.

This surprising result, however, only makes a final unsolved puzzle more vexing. Precisely who founded the fortified towns of Angel and Kincaid, and why? Clearly, these people had already embraced the Mississippian way of life; the close similarities between layouts and buildings in the two places demonstrate that their inhabitants shared Mississippian ideals concerning architecture and the use of space. Considering the towns' proximity to Cahokia, perhaps their founders had seen or even lived in Cahokia itself. Or perhaps they were local people who embraced only secondhand the array of Mississippian lifeways emanating out of greater Cahokia in the late 1000s. Either way, our magnetic surveys attest that these societal changes came with a prolonged threat of violence, exposing a darker side of medieval Mississippian life.

Staffan Peterson is interested in the relationships between social processes, architecture, and planning in large, pre-Columbian American Indian towns. He has conducted extensive research at the Angel, Kincaid, and Mann sites in the middle Ohio River valley and is the author of *Townscape Archaeology at Angel Mounds, Indiana: Mississippian Spatiality and Community* (2011). He is also park archaeologist for Yellowstone National Park.

Figure 12.1. Computer-generated scene showing how part of the Mississippian village of Upper Nodena, Arkansas, once looked. This visualization includes no palisade wall; compare with figure 12.6. Archaeologists are unsure whether a palisade existed or not.

Visualizing a Medieval Mississippian Town

Fred Limp, Snow Winters, and Angie Payne

Archaeologists normally describe ancient towns and villages by means of maps, written descriptions, charts, and diagrams. They may also use advanced technology such as LiDAR and magnetometry to visually reveal buildings, palisades, and causeways now lost to view. But as useful as these forms of description are, they seldom offer much sense of what an archaeological site looked like, on the ground, to people who lived in the place when it bustled with life.

A complementary way to convey the lived experiences of people of the past is to use computer visualization technologies. With enough information about a site and the right computer software, we can create realistic images of the way the settlement might once have appeared. We have done this for a small Mississippian town known to archaeologists as the Upper Nodena site.

Upper Nodena sits on a relict channel of the Mississippi River in present-day northeastern Arkansas. Flourishing between 1400 and 1600 CE, the town covered approximately fifteen and a half acres and housed an estimated one thousand to fifteen hundred residents. Its civic-ceremonial complex consisted of two platform mounds, a burial mound, and a modest plaza connecting the mounds. In the early twentieth century, James Hampson studied Upper Nodena extensively. Later, crews from the Universities of Alabama and Arkansas conducted excavations there. These

researchers found houses and cemeteries surrounding the ceremonial core of the small town, with the largest houses situated near the mounds.

Starting with what the earlier researchers had

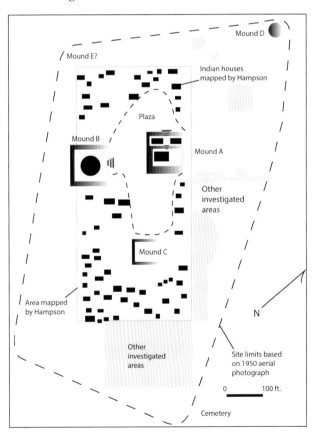

Figure 12.2. Plan of the Upper Nodena site, integrating results of field investigations by James Hampson, the University of Alabama, and the University of Arkansas.

Figure 12.3. Bird's-eye view of Upper Nodena and its agricultural fields.

learned, we first created a visualization of Upper Nodena as it might have looked from the air. Yet the hard archaeological data alone were not enough to fill out the scene. To make it more realistic, we needed information from other sources. For example, early historical records and botanical studies at other archaeological sites led us to believe that agricultural fields and groves of nut-bearing trees such as hickories and walnuts must have lain nearby. Anthropologists who studied midwestern American Indians in the late 1800s described how those people managed forests for nuts and game animals. By burning the underbrush, they enhanced the habitat for species such as deer, and by girdling non-nut-bearing trees to kill them, they kept nut-bearing trees isolated and therefore less susceptible to the loss of nuts to squirrels. When tree canopies are close together, squirrels move freely from treetop to treetop and leave few nuts to fall to the forest floor. But squirrels are reluctant to come down from the trees and cross open ground, so

nut harvests increase when surrounding trees—"squirrel bridges"—disappear.

We used knowledge like this, along with information about pre-Columbian fields gained from archaeological excavations, to decide how to depict the forest and fields surrounding Upper Nodena. We put the cornfields in places where modern soil maps show well-drained soils that are suitable for crops, and not on the poorly drained, swampy soils that cover much of the area. We knew from geological studies that the relict river channel east of the site still carried water at the time people lived there, so we showed it as a lake in the distance.

Mixing collateral information with firm archaeological evidence adds invaluable details to our visualizations, but it must be done with caution and good judgment. One of our researchers, for example, while working on a visualization of the interior of a home from around 1400, wondered whether he should depict any tables or other furniture in the house. We had no archaeological

Figure 12.4. Ceremonial structures atop Mound A.

evidence of furniture, but anthropological and historical sources describe later Native people using such objects. Our colleague had to decide which historically known furnishings, if any, could accurately be shown in a Mississippian house. Drawing on the historic and ethnographic sources, he added tables, shelving, and sleeping platforms, but in a way consistent with local decorative traditions.

For the visualizations illustrated in this chapter, we recorded the linkages between every element depicted and the sources from which we derived them. Interested readers are encouraged to review the bases for our decisions at http:// hampson.cast.uark.edu/nodena_3D_FAQ.htm.

As we moved from our bird's-eye view of Upper Nodena into the middle of the town, solid archaeological evidence about the locations of mounds and houses underpinned our computerized images.

Three rectangular wooden buildings, which we felt confident in depicting with thatched roofs, sat atop Mound A, making it a true architectural complex. On Mound B, the pattern of post holes showed that its single building was large and circular—a relatively unusual style. Near the center of the community plaza, between Mounds A and B, stood an upright wooden marker pole. Such mound-and-plaza combinations with marker poles are common in Mississippian archaeological sites, and early European explorers described them in eastern Native towns as well. Just the way many of our public buildings today are placed on pedestals and approached via stairs, so, too, were these Mississippian ceremonial and political buildings.

Many indigenous eastern North Americans built palisade walls around their towns, apparently to defend themselves and their temples. Whether or

Figure 12.5. The marker post in the town plaza, between the primary platform mounds.

not a palisade surrounded Upper Nodena is no settled matter; the archaeological evidence is so far somewhat ambiguous. If a palisade were present, how might it have changed people's experience of the town? As our visualization shows, a wall would have altered the way residents moved about in the town and across the landscape. It probably would have had a gate with a small opening, making defense easier but constraining the way people could leave or enter.

Of course people's experiences of Upper Nodena and all other medieval Mississippian places were flavored by far more than arrangements of palisades, pyramids, houses, and plazas. Among other things, ancient alignments and atmospherics must have played their part: haze, fog, the effects of the sun, the rising or setting of a full moon. Computer visualization software enables us to get a sense of how, for instance, Upper Nodena might have appeared on a summer evening as the sun was setting (plate 20). What did the people think as their skin felt the last rays of the sun on an autumn day, with flocks of geese in the distance and children's laughter in the yards of houses? Through our visualizations we hope to move, carefully, a bit closer to the rich and complex human experiences behind our maps, artifacts, and impersonal data.

Figure 12.6. Visualization of a palisade encircling Upper Nodena, with a narrow entrance, or gate. On the left, a house is under construction.

Fred Limp holds the Leica Geo-systems Chair and is a University Professor in the Department of Geosciences at the University of Arkansas, Fayetteville. He has been involved in the application of computer and geospatial technologies in archaeology for more than three decades.

Snow Winters and **Angie Payne** both work at the Center for Advanced Spatial Technologies at the University of Arkansas. Winters is involved in creating three-dimensional visualizations of the past and present in Arkansas and elsewhere; among her most notable projects is a visualization of Machu Picchu, Peru. Payne's research interests include 3D scanning applications and historic and archaeological visualization. She managed the Upper Nodena Village Visualizations project.

Figure 13.1. An array of Mississippian stone tools.

Crafting the Medieval Landscape with Stone Tools

Brad H. Koldehoff

With nothing more than digging sticks, baskets, and stone-bladed axes and hoes, medieval Mississippians transformed floodplain forests and prairies across the midcontinent into agricultural, urban, and ritual landscapes. Nowhere is this more apparent than at Cahokia, where, seemingly overnight, people leveled a nearly fifty-acre central plaza and ringed it with Monks Mound, the largest earthen structure in the New World, and more than a hundred other earthen monuments. Ritual marker posts the size of modern telephone poles went up across the site, and a defensive wall composed of an estimated twenty thousand posts encircled the city center. How did the Cahokians, and other Mississippians after them, accomplish such things—not to mention the myriad ordinary tasks of constructing houses and canoes, hunting and butchering animals, and tilling and weeding fields—with modest tools of wood and stone?

Technologically the Mississippians, like most indigenous groups before the arrival of Europeans, were "stone age" people—however medieval they might otherwise seem. Their only metal objects were flashy ornaments hammered from nuggets of native copper from around the Great Lakes. But the label "stone age" does not mean they were unsophisticated folk. To the contrary, it means they used stone tools to achieve great things. Like the Mayas in Mesoamerica, they mined and worked a flintlike rock called chert into heavy-duty, uniform tool

blades that they fitted with wooden handles and used in farming, landscaping, mound building, woodworking, and mining. With sturdy, beautifully polished basalt ax heads they felled trees. A master craftsperson could work these common raw materials, as well as more unusual minerals such as mica and the soft red stone known as flint clay, into finely made items that people displayed to convey social status or spiritual beliefs. For example, master stoneworkers skillfully chipped large chert nodules into long, thin ceremonial weapons that archaeologists call maces, swords, and daggers.

Mississippians employed two methods of stoneworking: chipping and a combination of pecking and grinding. They knew well which kinds of stone ensured the best performance in which kinds of tools. Ax heads, which needed to be heavy and fracture resistant, required basalt or some other igneous rock quarried from the St. Francois Mountains in the Missouri Ozarks. Workers pried and hammered slabs of such stone from outcroppings and then chipped the slabs into roughly shaped, unfinished ax heads. To finish shaping, sharpening, and polishing a single ax head required many hours, if not days, spent pecking the piece with a small chert hammerstone and grinding it with a slab of sandstone.

For the blades of hoes and woodworking tools such as adzes and chisels, Mississippian stoneworkers along the lower Ohio and central Mississippi

Figure 13.2. Mississippian stone ax heads. The longest piece shown here, measuring fourteen inches long, is unfinished.

River valleys preferred coarse-grained cherts. They routinely selected a kind now called Mill Creek chert, from southern Illinois, from which to chip these large tools, because it occurs in long, flat nodules and because its coarse texture yields sharp, durable edges, more fracture resistant than edges flaked from finer-grained cherts. For similar reasons, artisans favored Dover chert, from Tennessee, for large flaked tool blades and even the occasional ax head. Other popular kinds of stone for sharp blades were Kaolin chert, a tough and colorful material with sources near Mill Creek in southern Illinois, and Crescent chert, from the northeastern edge of the Missouri Ozarks.

Quarries in the Mill Creek, Dover, Kaolin, and Crescent source areas furnished Mississippians and earlier groups with almost endless supplies of chert blocks and nodules, if they were willing to dig for them. Mississippian miners sank pits and shafts into hilltops and ridge slopes to retrieve buried stone. In 1919 the anthropologist William Henry Holmes wrote of the Mill Creek quarries, where

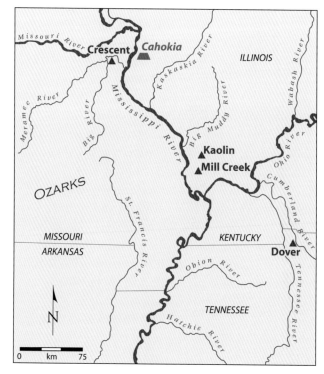

Figure 13.3. Locations of major chert quarries in the middle Mississippi Valley.

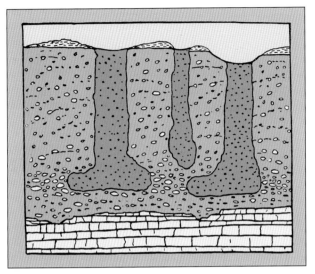

Figure 13.4. Schematic view of the Mill Creek chert quarry pits. Miners dug shafts into soil laden with chert nodules until they nearly reached bedrock. Piles of debris lie on the surface between the shafts.

Figure 13.5. Flakes of Crescent chert struck from a quarried block (*bottom center*) with a hammerstone (*left*). Such flakes served for many household tasks.

shafts reached twenty-five feet deep, that "the magnitude of the ancient work is almost beyond belief." Quarries served as classrooms, too, where apprentice stoneworkers received training in the technically demanding skills they needed to make large blades flaked expertly on both sides to thin and shape them.

Recent experiments in stone tool production have revealed the different levels of skill required to make different kinds of Mississippian tools. At one extreme, a person needed little skill to quickly chip a sharp flake from a block of chert to use for cutting, scraping, and other routine tasks. At Cahokia, households kept a hammerstone and a chunk of chert from the nearby Crescent quarry handy as a standard tool kit. Family members would strike off a flake tool, use it a few times, and then discard it when the edge dulled.

At the middle level, pecking and grinding a block of dense stone into an ax head called for some skill and a lot more patience. Pecking with a chert hammer and grinding with a sandstone slab are time consuming but need relatively little training and practice. Stone-grinding workshops are nearly invisible on the landscape, because failure was uncommon and waste products were few—a handful of flakes and some rock dust. At a stone

source, one or a few persons probably extracted a block and roughly shaped it into the beginnings of an ax, which someone else finished at another location. I think it likely that the people who finished and then used and maintained the ax heads were community experts, probably local woodcutters.

At the most skilled extreme, manufacturing specialized tools such as hoe blades demanded years of training and constant practice. Making a tool as large as a hoe blade is risky. The stoneworker must strike at least thirty carefully placed blows with an antler hammer on both sides of the emerging tool, removing large flakes and thinning the piece without snapping it. Opportunities for failure abound. Stone-chipping workshops around the Mill Creek and Dover quarries are littered with failed and rejected blades and enormous piles of waste flakes. With training and practice, however—and keen familiarity with the local stone—a skilled stoneworker learned to reduce large nodules of chert into effective tool blades. The most accomplished stoneworkers crafted long, thin, elegantly shaped ceremonial maces and swords used during certain rituals.

While Mississippians made simple flake tools and probably finished ax heads right at home, they got their large chert blades ready-made from distant workshops. The reason lies in a combination of economy and environment. Because Mississippians were farmers, they lived in and along major river valleys, far from most important stone sources. Cahokia, for instance, sits in a broad, sediment-filled valley with fertile topsoils amenable to hoe agriculture but with few rock outcrops. Yet the corn-farming Mississippians needed steady supplies of ax heads and hoe blades for clearing and cultivating fields, not to mention building houses, mounds, plazas, and temples. Raw stone, whether for hearths or hoe blades, had to be mined in the surrounding uplands.

The demands of farming, though, kept most members of Mississippian households close to home. They had little time to travel back and forth to quarries and so found few opportunities to learn and practice the skills needed to mine and shape stone into hoe and adze blades. Instead, it was people who lived near quarries who became miners and skilled stoneworkers. In habitation sites we find ample evidence for the use of hoes, but only at quarry-related sites do we see the waste flakes that attest to hoe production. Clearly, quarry-based stoneworkers were production specialists.

The distance between population centers and quarries created economic opportunities for both stoneworkers and town dwellers, who developed trading partnerships to move finished tools from quarries to river-valley towns and on to scattered farming villages. Town leaders and entrepreneurs no doubt profited from the trade and perhaps even controlled local access to vital tools. Up and down the central Mississippi and lower Ohio valleys, we find stockpiles of hoe blades, sometimes dozens of tools at a time. Such caches turn up primarily at mound centers, where these important tools were secreted in underground pits or in mounds for safe-keeping. Perhaps some of them served as offerings to fallen leaders and to ancestors.

Mississippians living in the central valley north of the Ohio River, especially residents of greater Cahokia, formed trading partnerships with quarry folk near the Mill Creek and Kaolin chert sources, which lay a relatively short canoe journey down the Mississippi. Consumers in this northern area used large blade tools made of Mill Creek chert to the near exclusion of tools manufactured at the Dover quarries in present-day Tennessee. Conversely, consumers south of the Ohio Valley, nearer the Dover source, relied heavily on tools from Dover chert workshops. In between those two consumer regions, along the lower Ohio River itself, blades made from both Mill Creek and Dover chert commonly turn up in archaeological sites.

Although distances and ease of travel between consumers and producers may be the main reasons behind the north-south divide, residents of each of the two big consumer regions might also have been united through political alliances or shared cultural identities. I say this because tool blades of Mill Creek and Dover chert look different from each other. In most cases, a quick glance would have told an observer which quarry and workshop a tool came from and therefore whether or not the user was "one of us."

For one thing, Dover chert is much darker brown than Mill Creek chert (plates 15 and 16), so the color of a tool was an instant giveaway. For another, stoneworkers in the two workshops made tools of distinctively different styles and shapes. The only chert worked into ax heads, for example, was the Dover variety, and correspondingly, those axes served users along the Ohio Valley and southward. North of the Ohio, people generally used ax heads ground from basalt. Meanwhile, only the Mill Creek and Kaolin workshops produced hoe blades with notches at one end for ease of tying the blade to the wooden handle. Notched hoe blades, predictably, appear almost exclusively north of the Ohio River. The same is true of a type of knife blade or dagger known as the Ramey knife, and ceremonial swords and maces took slightly different shapes in the Mill Creek and Dover workshops. Together, such differences reflect the practices of two communities of skilled stoneworkers who, while sharing similar technologies and Mississippian beliefs, were linked to different consumer populations. Intentionally or not, those consumers might have seen "their" tools, made at "their" workshops and obtained from "their" traders, as expressions of their identity.

Stone tools, then, helped give material shape to social and political relationships in the medieval

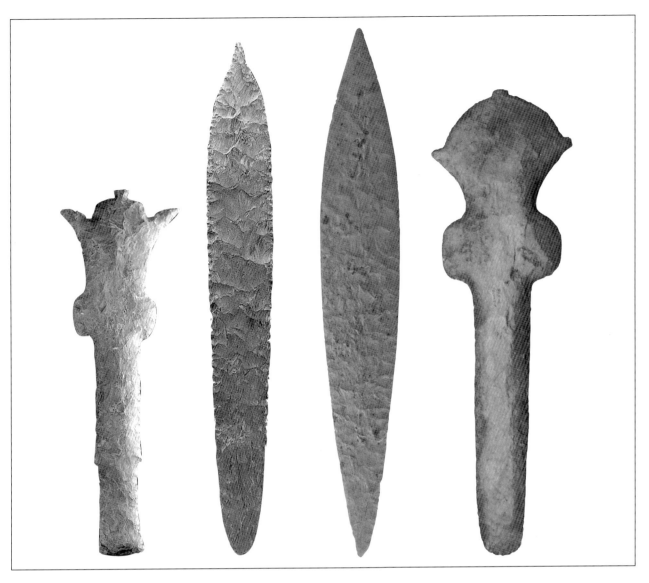

Figure 13.6. Mississippian ceremonial weapons. *From left*: mace and sword made from Dover chert; sword and mace made from Mill Creek chert. Mace at right is fifteen inches long.

Mississippian world, even as they helped physically shape that world. With stone tools the Mississippians accomplished remarkable things, especially at Cahokia. No one in ancient North America moved more dirt and cut more timber than did the Cahokians, and they achieved their extraordinary accomplishments by wielding axes and hoes with stone blades.

Brad H. Koldehoff is the chief archaeologist for the Illinois Department of Transportation. For the past thirty-five years he has conducted investigations in the central Mississippi Valley and studied the stone tools used by the ancient peoples of that region.

Figure 14.1. Broken pots on a burned house floor at the Crable site in the central Illinois River valley.

Incinerated Villages in the North

fourteen

Greg D. Wilson

It is summer in the central Illinois River valley in the year 1238 CE. A small, bluff-top village is under attack by an overwhelming force gathered from allied enemy villages. Archers man the palisade wall, and men, women, and children scramble in all directions as the attackers' first flaming arrows hit the thatched roofs of the villagers' homes.

Life in this valley during the 1200s meant living with the threat of assault always just over the horizon. The archaeological discovery of burned villages all over the region tells us that organized attacks were real concerns. At the peak of hostilities, a village might have suffered devastating assaults several times in a generation. Many of the valley's inhabitants must have lost friends or family members to the violence. The looming threat of attack appears to have affected everything from chiefly leaders' political relationships with Cahokians to the way commoners fished, farmed, and hunted.

The central Illinois River valley is a 130-mile segment of the Illinois River running from the modern town of Meredosia, in Morgan County, Illinois, northeastward to Hennepin, in Putnam County. Mississippianized people lived in the valley from around 1100 CE until about 1450, when the whole region was abandoned. During the decades of violence that started around 1200, Mississippians in this area built most of their villages on defensible bluff crests on the western side of the valley. There, the bluffs usually rise well over a hundred feet

above the valley floor and in places are cut into sharp ridges by the valleys of small streams draining the adjacent country.

From their bluff-top redoubts, villagers would have been able to keep watch over great swathes of the valley floor, hindering their enemies' attempts to launch surprise offensives. And any assault force approaching a fortified town from the valley below would have faced a precarious charge up a steep incline while dodging volleys of arrows fired by archers positioned strategically along wooden palisade walls. Yet despite the high risks associated with attack, many offensives succeeded. At least five and perhaps as many as ten fortified Mississippian settlements in the central Illinois River valley ended in flames, apparently having been set ablaze during large-scale, direct assaults or after sudden, strategic abandonments.

For archaeologists, these catastrophic burnings created a rare "Pompeii-like" snapshot of ancient life in the region, a well-preserved picture of settlements where fleeing residents left whole pots, stone tools, and ritual objects in place on dwelling floors. Much about the hostilities that produced such a record of devastation remains a mystery. The story of what we do know begins just before violence escalated in the region.

In the centuries before Cahokia and the appearance of the first Mississippians in the central Illinois River valley, at least two Late Woodland groups

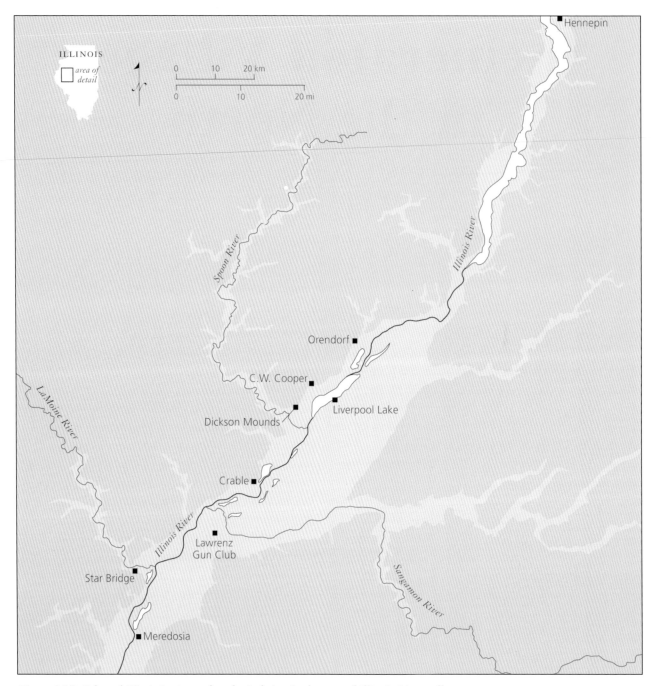

Figure 14.2. Selected Mississippian archaeological sites in the central Illinois River valley.

lived there, making different styles of pottery and erecting their villages in different kinds of places. Increasingly at the time, groups throughout the American midcontinent were becoming more permanently settled, staking claims to their own pieces of the landscape and investing more heavily in growing seed crops. Violence must have erupted among them occasionally, for archaeologists sometimes find graves holding group burials and skeletons with arrow or spear points embedded in the bones. But no valley residents of this era fortified their settlements, so hostilities must have been small-scale and relatively rare.

In the mid-1000s, the founding and expansion of Cahokia more than a hundred river miles to the south sent political and religious shock waves through tribal societies in the Midwest, South, and Great Plains. People of the central Illinois River

Figure 14.3. Burned cross-shaped temple at the Eveland site.

valley almost immediately began emulating Cahokian ways of making and decorating pots and building houses.

A second pulse of Cahokian influence and emulation began around 1100, corresponding to the beginning of Cahokia's "classic" period. Mississippianized residents of the central Illinois Valley now erected Cahokia-style temples in at least two small ceremonial sites. The better understood of these is Eveland, where excavators uncovered seven Mississippian structures. Four of the structures were Cahokia-style temples—a cross-shaped building built over an earlier rectangular one, a large T-shaped building, and a circular sweat lodge. The Eveland site stood adjacent to the other ceremonial site, Dickson Mounds mortuary complex, where 250 people were interred during the early 1100s. Among the burials were four decapitated adult men, buried together with pottery vessels positioned in place of their heads. Their ritual execution and burial were nearly identical to an earlier sacrificial event at Cahokia, in which four adult men whose heads and hands had been severed were collectively buried under the ridge-top Mound 72.

The Cahokia-style human sacrifice and the well-developed temple and mortuary complex at Eveland and Dickson Mounds imply that Cahokian religion played an important part in the Mississippianization of the central Illinois River valley in the early 1100s. People of the valley also emulated Cahokian material culture more pervasively at this time. Although traces of Woodland-style living persisted, visitors to any settlement in the central valley would have met people living in Cahokia-style wall-trench houses, cooking and storing food in Cahokia-style pots, and hunting with Cahokia-style arrowheads. Perhaps by adopting a relatively uniform array of Cahokian material forms, groups in the region downplayed their long-standing ethnic divisions.

In any event, this period of Cahokian influence and emulation lasted no more than fifty years before people dramatically scaled back their connections to Cahokia or even severed them entirely. Marking this transition was the planned and complete abandonment of the Eveland site: all ritual items were removed from its temples, and its buildings were burned. The deliberate termination of Eveland corresponded

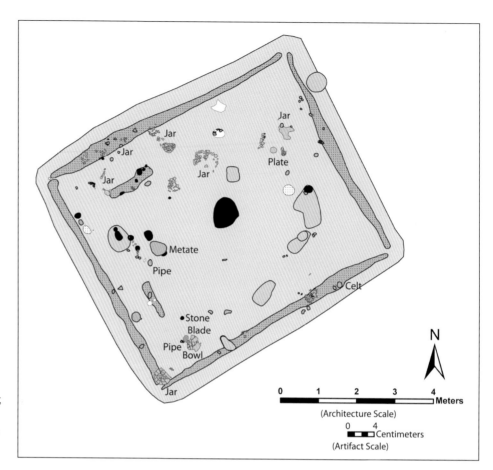

Figure 14.4. Artifacts left on a burned house floor at the Orendorf site, including pottery vessels used for cooking, storage, and serving; a large sandstone *metate*, or corn-grinding stone; and two stone tobacco pipes.

roughly to a series of burning events at Cahokia-affiliated Mississippian sites in the lower Illinois River valley and in Cahokia's East St. Louis precinct. Political turmoil was roiling the greater Cahokia area and quickly spilled over into neighboring regions. The result was village-against-village violence.

Following the ritual burning of Eveland in the mid-1100s, people in the central valley began for the first time to establish compact villages set on defensible bluff edges and protected by wooden palisades. By 1200, much of the regional populace had settled into and around such villages. The best understood of them is the Orendorf site. From this bluff-top perch, residents of five sequentially occupied villages, spanning the final century of the Woodland era through the Mississippian period, looked down over the western valley floor. Orendorf's last manifestation consisted of a twelve-acre palisaded settlement with an estimated four hundred to five hundred inhabitants. This village underwent two episodes of expansion; each time, the palisade wall was rebuilt. Designed for military purposes, the wall featured bastions regularly

Figure 14.5. Aerial view of Star Bridges, a burned Mississippian village in the central Illinois River valley dating to the 1200s. The striations visible in this photo and figure 14.6 are plow furrows.

spaced at intervals corresponding to the effective range of a bow and arrow.

Finally, around 1250, this final Orendorf village burned to the ground. Residents left rapidly and without planning, abandoning whole pots, valuable

Figure 14.6. Aerial view of Buckeye Bend, a burned Mississippian village in the central Illinois River valley dating to the 1200s.

tools, and ritual paraphernalia intact where they sat on house floors. They even left behind the body of a recently deceased man, unburied in a burned house. And Orendorf was not alone; widespread burning razed other villages in the central valley in the late 1200s. Aerial photographs of two such sites—Buckeye Bend and Star Bridges—reveal rows of densely packed, burned houses arranged around rectangular central plazas. The thoroughness of the burning and the abandonment of intact domestic possessions declare the most likely cause to have been warfare.

Certainly, the palisades surrounding villages in the 1200s were designed to keep unwanted persons out. Ironically, the risk of attack appears also to have kept people inside the walls. Life in the fortified villages was crowded. People who had once moved easily about the countryside, traveling to distant fields and hunting grounds, now found their movement constrained, and the transformation proved costly. For example, recent research on skeletal remains from the central valley shows that the move into fortified villages damaged women's health and lowered their life expectancy. During pregnancy and shortly afterward, women are especially susceptible to harmful viruses and bacteria, which would have flourished and been easily transmitted from person to person in densely packed villages.

Chronic warfare also obstructed the daily food quest. Community members had to reorganize their diet in order to minimize the risk of attack while fishing, farming, and hunting. Archaeological studies of Mississippian foodways are revealing that community members in the central Illinois Valley coped by concentrating on growing maize at the expense of pursuits such as gathering wild plants and fishing, which required frequent or lengthy trips away from home. The result of these violence-induced changes was a narrower, less nutritious diet that was more vulnerable to shortfalls.

Of course the most obvious cost of living with chronic warfare—whether one was victim or attacker—was injury or death. Orendorf saw an adult trauma rate higher than that known for any other Mississippian territory in eastern North America. Violence-related deaths there included more than fifteen people buried in a mass grave and numerous others with embedded arrow points, scalping cuts, and blunt force trauma to the skull. Males and females above the age of twelve appear to have been targeted equally.

Into this hornet's nest of fortified, warring settlements came a cultural group known archaeologically as the Oneota people, relocating from somewhere in the northern Midwest around 1300. The precise genetic or blood relationships between the Oneota immigrants and local Mississippians are unclear. But coinciding with the Oneotas' arrival, some Mississippian villagers shifted their settlements ten to twenty miles southward, abandoning the area around the confluence of the Spoon River and the Illinois River. Their relocation intimates antagonism between the two groups, yet archaeologists have uncovered a mixture of Oneota and Mississippian ceramic vessels in household refuse at Oneota and Mississippian sites dating to the 1300s, which might hint at alliances. Alternatively, the intermixture of pottery might mean that captive women and children were held in rival villages. In this scenario, captives taken in raids continued to make cooking and serving containers using their own stylistic conventions, even while living among the opposing group.

Adopting captives to replace deceased family members was a common practice among American Indians in parts of the war-torn Midwest and South from the 1500s through the 1800s. Sometimes these captives had low status or lived socially marginalized lives. Evidence tentatively suggesting captive-taking in the central Illinois River valley comes from the Crable site. There, people normally laid their dead to rest with great care in spacious cemeteries, sometimes placing elaborate artifacts with them. In the residential portion of the site, however, excavators uncovered the skeleton of a woman in her early twenties who, in the early 1400s, had been haphazardly dumped into an abandoned storage pit and covered with household trash. The callous manner in which this young woman's body was treated tells us that she was of exceedingly low social status in the Crable community, perhaps because of her identity as a captive.

Like captive-taking, with its scant evidence, much else that we would like to know about late Mississippian life in the central Illinois Valley remains sketchy. We cannot yet answer fundamental questions such as who, exactly, allied with whom and fought with whom—and why they fought in the first place. What can be said with certainty is that these people, at the very end of the Medieval Warm Period, lived with and were fundamentally changed by war.

During the 1400s and into the 1500s, a string of decade-long droughts in the central valley ravaged villagers' maize harvests. Food shortages must have been severe for the inhabitants of fortified villages, who had to farm within running distance of their palisade walls. Skeletal evidence shows unambiguously that the risk of venturing away from home surged after 1300. Excavations in fortified villages have revealed the remains of many bodies that, after lying exposed to the elements for some time, were finally found and brought home for burial.

When a particularly catastrophic drought struck around 1450, family after family began streaming out of the central valley. Indeed, the severity of this drought may also have been a reason for the nearly contemporaneous abandonment of parts of the greater Cahokia region and of the area around the confluence of the Mississippi and Ohio Rivers to the south. The Mississippian and Oneota inhabitants of the central Illinois River valley left, their descendants becoming members of Indian tribes such as the Omaha, Osage, and Iowa. Today, their homelands lie to the south and west of Illinois.

Greg D. Wilson is an associate professor at the University of California, Santa Barbara, whose archaeological research concerns social inequality, identity politics, and violence in pre-Columbian North and South America. His perspective is informed by contemporary theoretical research into human agency, practice, and political economy. He investigates these issues through a household- and community-centered archaeology with an emphasis on methodologically rigorous analyses of large and diverse data sets.

Figure 15.1. A reconstruction of SunWatch village along the Great Miami River, with Dayton, Ohio, in the background. Some houses have been rebuilt on the site; others in this image, along with the palisade, are computer generated.

Mississippians in a Foreign Land

Robert Cook

In their farthest reach into northeastern North America, Mississippians moved into the middle Ohio River valley, in the modern states of Indiana, Kentucky, Ohio, and West Virginia, where they lived among people whom archaeologists call the Fort Ancient culture. Fort Ancient people were not often Mississippians themselves; they were Late Woodland descendants of the mound-building Hopewell culture in the region who mixed with Mississippians. Mississippian ways came to these folk at the inception of Fort Ancient culture, just as the great city of Cahokia was forming and influencing people far and wide. Recent research is proving Fort Ancient culture to be a good example of the way Mississippian beliefs, styles, and individual persons affected foreigners far from the Mississippi River heartland.

By archaeologists' reckoning, Fort Ancient culture emerged in the middle Ohio Valley in the late 1000s and the 1100s—the same time the first Mississippian towns were developing to the south and west. From the start, Fort Ancient people lived in large villages and grew corn on a par with many other Mississippians. They also hunted deer, fished, and gathered wild plants. Their initial interactions with Mississippians appear to have included gift exchanges and marriage alliances and were closely tied to the intensification of maize farming and village beginnings.

The Mississippian part of the Fort Ancient story began, for me, with a house. In piecing together maps of one well-excavated Fort Ancient village,

now called SunWatch, I noticed that one house there was different from all the others. Unlike traditional Fort Ancient houses, whose wall posts were set in individually dug holes, this one had been built in the typical Mississippian style, with wall trenches. Its builders had also set it much closer to the village center than the other houses. Could this really have been a Mississippian house? Had foreigners somehow factored into local developments at SunWatch? I wanted to know more.

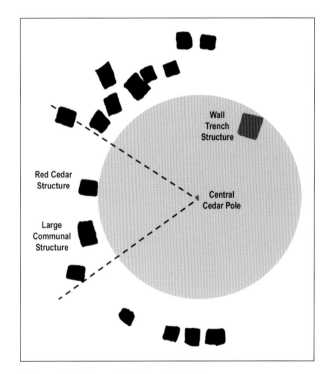

Figure 15.2. Plan of the SunWatch site.

To reconstruct the village's history from the 1100s through the 1400s, I put together old and new radiocarbon dates, looked at patterns of house rebuilding at the site, and examined artifacts for styles characteristic of different time periods. Well into the 1200s, I found, only about half the number of houses eventually built in the village were in use, and no special buildings or artifacts clearly signaled the presence of leaders or public rituals. By the late 1300s, the situation had changed. Now I could detect leaders among the burials at the site, along with unusual buildings—the wall-trench house, a large communal building, and a red cedar structure in the west, positioned between solstice solar alignments associated with a large, centrally placed cedar post. All these traits are hallmarks of Mississippian villages.

Fort Ancient people often buried their dead around the edges of their village plazas, and the residents of SunWatch were no exception. With the twentieth-century passage of federal and state laws protecting Native burials, they are seldom excavated nowadays, but museums in southern Ohio curate previously excavated human remains. Having been granted permission to study human bones in museums, in cooperation with American Indians, I was quickly able to recognize a SunWatch village leader. A man in his thirties, he had been buried with a whelk shell pendant, a common status symbol in Mississippian communities. His grave was connected in time with the Mississippian-style wall-trench house and lay next to the red cedar structure. Nearby, other men had been laid to rest who, judging from the objects accompanying them, were also prominent in the village. But was the leader with the whelk pendant a local man, or did he come from a distant Mississippian community? My colleagues and I are currently conducting biological and chemical studies to better establish where he and others at SunWatch and other villages were born. At this point, it is clear that "outsiders" were buried at several villages, but where they came from is still being investigated.

I like to think of the man with the whelk shell as a "peace chief" because, unlike some other men buried at SunWatch, he lacked any evidence of human conflict. Other burials might be candidates

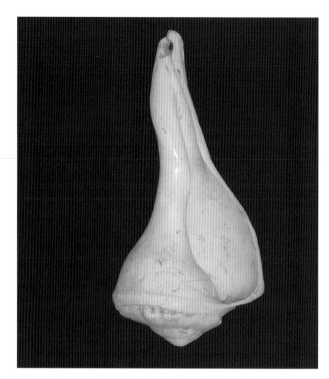

Figure 15.3. A Mississippian whelk shell pendant, five inches long.

for "war chiefs." One man in his twenties had suffered a fatal blow to the back of his skull. He was also one of a small group of adult males who had each been buried with a cut and polished wolf jaw, objects denoting their special status. Most of the other men, too, showed signs of the kinds of trauma fighters receive in battle. At SunWatch, perhaps the local Fort Ancient people courted distant Mississippians to come and help with increasing warfare during the 1400s. At the least, they might have wanted aid in bolstering the development of leadership in their growing community.

Researchers now know that SunWatch was far from alone among Fort Ancient villages in displaying Mississippian traits. More than a dozen sites, mostly concentrated in southwest Ohio, have been discovered to have wall-trench houses. Excavators have uncovered artifacts made in the Mississippian heartland, among them large stone knives or swords made from high-quality materials such as Kaolin chert, from southern Illinois. Archaeologists working nearer Cahokia sometimes call these "Ramey knives." I know of three Fort Ancient villages that have Ramey knives or blades in related styles. One

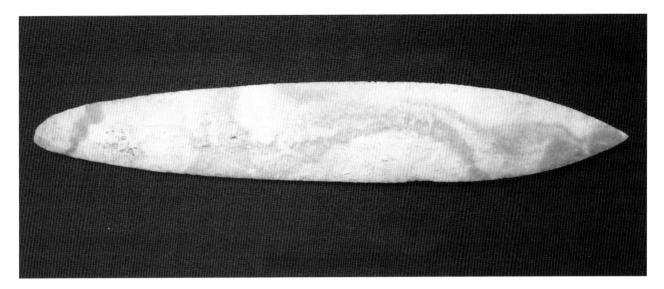

Figure 15.4. A Ramey knife, thirteen inches long.

of those villages sat at the mouth of the Great Miami River, downriver from SunWatch and relatively close to the nearest Mississippian sources. There, a previous excavation had revealed the remains of a man buried with the Ramey knife in his right hand. My colleagues and I recently began to investigate this village. After just a few days of magnetic survey, it became clear that the overall pattern of houses strongly resembled that at SunWatch but preceded it by a generation or more. I am now leading excavations at this site to learn more about it.

Medieval Mississippians left their marks on Fort Ancient culture, although researchers have so far only scratched the surface in learning exactly how and why the two peoples interacted. The middle Ohio River valley was one of many areas into which these foreigners came, and as they did everywhere, they profoundly affected receptive local people who were becoming maize-farming villagers at the same time.

Robert Cook is an associate professor in the Department of Anthropology at Ohio State University. His recent research has been focused on human mobility, prehistoric architecture, monumentality, and Mississippian origins, within broader interests in household archaeology, mortuary studies, taxonomy, and ethnic complexity. He is the author of *SunWatch: Fort Ancient Development in the Mississippian World* (2008).

Figure 16.1. Donna Rausch excavating a hearth in Mound A at Shiloh National Military Park, Tennessee.

Being Chickasaw at Shiloh

sixteen

Donna J. Rausch

I came from the west. I sit on top of the mound and watch the sun rise in the east, its golden light spreading across the plaza and sparkling on the Tennessee River below. I am not supposed to be here. I have driven through the night to reach the mound early, very early in the morning. I have told no one. I am expected to arrive here, at Shiloh National Military Park, in several days to work as an archaeological technician on the Shiloh Mound project. But before starting as a crew member, I want to connect with the mound site by myself, as a Chickasaw. For now I will sit peacefully, breathe deeply, and let the mound's essence surround me— the essence of the past and of a place where my ancestors might have walked.

Starting in 2001 and continuing for three field seasons, the National Park Service's Southeast Archeological Center conducted excavations at Mound A, the temple mound, of the Shiloh mound complex in Shiloh National Military Park. Mississippian people lived at this group of seven imposing mounds arranged around a plaza from about 1050 to 1350 CE. They built their town on a high bluff overlooking the Tennessee River, and in its heyday it was surrounded by a great wooden palisade wall. In recent times the mound and adjoining areas of the Shiloh complex have been eroding into the river, which was one of the reasons behind the Park Service's dig.

Oral traditions tell Native American people

where they came from. I grew up with stories of Chickasaw arrival in the East from the West. My great-great-great-great-great-grandmother Molly Colbert Oxberry Gunn told a version of the Chickasaw migration story that is still told today in the Chickasaw Nation. It recounts how, in the distant past, the Chickasaw crossed the Mississippi River from an earlier home in the West. Their first settlement east of the river was Chickasaw Old Fields, on the Tennessee River. By 1700 Chickasaw Old Fields had been moved southwest to the headwaters of the Tombigbee River in northeastern Mississippi, the Chickasaw's homeland during the historic period. The Chickasaw also controlled western Tennessee and Kentucky west of the divide

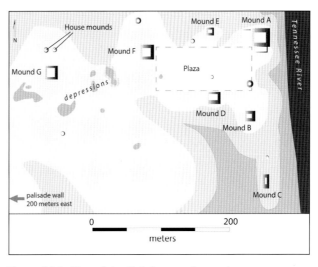

Figure 16.2. Plan of the Shiloh mound complex.

111

between the Cumberland and Tennessee Rivers. They ceded the Mississippi land east of the Tennessee River by treaty in 1816 and the land west of the Tennessee River, in the Shiloh area, by a treaty signed in October 1818.

Before doing archaeological work on public land, the National Park Service consults with the area's descendant tribe or tribes, especially about sensitive and legally protected finds such as burials. For Shiloh National Military Park, that tribe is the Chickasaw Nation. After reviewing and revising several proposals, representatives of the Chickasaw Nation and the Park Service met face-to-face on June 22, 2001, and negotiated a final research plan. Now the field season could begin.

As a graduate student in anthropology at the University of Mississippi and as a member of the Chickasaw Nation, I thought it seemed right, when offered the opportunity to work at Shiloh, to go back to my roots and see what the mound had to tell me. Yet I was concerned about my decision, because many Native American tribes today are reluctant to deal with archaeologists. Often, elders object, saying, "Our tribal sacred lands are all that remain to keep us connected to our place on Mother Earth. The lands and sacred places, what is left of them, connect us to our spirituality and our heritage. If archaeologists and looters take it all away, what will remain except a vague memory of a forgotten past?" Chickasaw, Choctaw, and other southeastern Indians say, "The mounds are sacred structures; to us they are holy places."

I went into the Shiloh Mound project with those words in mind and with mixed emotions— emotions that arise every time I think about what I do when I put a trowel to the ground. I knew that many tribal members disapproved of anthropologists and archaeologists, whom they perceived to be unconcerned with the way Native Americans feel and to be researching and writing books and articles merely to gain recognition for themselves and their college departments. Several of my fellow Chickasaw had confronted me over my interest in archaeology—an interest I had felt since childhood—and accused me of selling out my ancestors, of digging and disturbing burials.

I knew I was not selling out my heritage or my people. Like many others of Native American descent, I was taking a stand, determined to learn more about my tribal history instead of being disturbed by those who were writing it. I knew that many tribal members believed anthropologists had rewritten Native Americans' stories and oral traditions in ways that had reshaped the understanding of our collective past. In order to recapture the viewpoints of Native Americans, many scholars of Native ancestry had gone to college, earned degrees, and looked to new sources of evidence in anthropology, archaeology, and ethnohistory—evidence including oral traditions, material remains, and legal records. Together with like-minded non-Native scholars, they have redefined Native American history by adding previously overlooked points of view. Many tribes today, among them the Chickasaw Nation, even have their own archaeology and preservation offices, conducting research on their own terms.

I went into the Shiloh Mound project full of hope that the relationship between archaeologists and Native Americans could be made smoother. Communication and understanding of each other's views need to come first. In the past, archaeologists did not always talk to those whose ancestors they studied and often came away with misunderstandings of what they had seen. Rarely did they take into account the effect their research might have on the people they studied. Native Americans, for their part, were not always quick to share information, because they distrusted the people asking the questions, for good reason. Today, we need to work together to right the wrongs of the past. That the Chickasaw Nation was willing to work with archaeologists on the Shiloh Mound project was a big step toward fixing the problem.

As the day drew nearer for me to leave for Shiloh, many people confronted me about my desire to work there. I knew, though, that the mound was eroding into the Tennessee River and we Chickasaw were at risk of losing any information it had to give us about our past. I believe the knowledge that comes from archaeology can help us discover more about our ancestors and add to our sense of who we are as a nation. We need to understand the amazing things our ancestors accomplished. The project at Shiloh was a quest for an answer: How did we get to where we are today?

For me personally, the quest was also about finding me—about finding a connection, a unifying element, between me and my people from the past. It was a quest to get closer to my history, and not just in words on paper. It was a quest to prove parts of the oral traditions that many of us of Native American descent were raised with or taught.

On the morning of July 10, 2001, I approached the mound again from the west, facing east in great anticipation. I walked with other archaeological techs toward the largest mound in the complex, through what would have been the town's plaza. We talked and laughed in excitement about what we might discover. As I walked, I imagined what it would have been like in the past. The sounds of early morning activities: people waking, women cooking over their hearths, children laughing, crying, playing, and men heading off to hunt. Or maybe everyone was facing east, looking toward the temple mound, waiting for the leader to appear and welcome the day.

On my first day I could sense caution toward me among some of the other crew members. Many of them were students, like me, in anthropology programs, but no one else was a member of a federally recognized tribe such as the Chickasaw Nation. Some believed I was there as a "token Indian," and a few wondered if I were a spy, there only to observe and report back to the tribe. Also on the first day a group of Boy Scouts visited the site. As I listened to the questions they asked and how they were answered, I soon realized that to the visitors and even to some of the crew, the people who had lived at the mound were "others," or "they," a people who no longer existed—not a living, growing population with rich, enduring cultural traditions, as I knew Native Americans to be.

So began the lessons I had come to learn and in some small way help my fellow crew members to understand. Every night I asked myself whether I was committed enough to face the crew the next day. Did I want to know and share my history enough, or to prove that I was there to work and learn just like them? As an anthropology student I knew that diversity and understanding of other worldviews were important, and we should strive to be less ethnocentric. As the days passed, I steadily began to earn the respect and friendship of the crew. The first field season was a time of proving myself to others and gaining acceptance simply as a valued member of the crew, not as a Chickasaw.

We found much that first season that enlightened me about the people who once lived at Shiloh. For example, layers of soil in the colors red and white kept showing up as we excavated, each colored soil specially selected from natural deposits nearby and stacked atop the others in layer-cake fashion (plate 19). The color red intrigued me, because for Native American people it is one of the sacred colors. Among many southeastern Indians, red symbolized, in the words of anthropologist Charles Hudson, "conflict, war, fear, disunity, and danger." White symbolized "that which is old, established, pure, peaceable, holy, [and] united." Red and white were also associated with kinship groups such as clans and with social divisions such as whole towns. I was also interested in the evidence we uncovered from the American Civil War. Shiloh's temple mound, a strategic height overlooking the Tennessee River, had served soldiers in the war just as it once served Native Americans—as a vantage point from which to watch the river and protect the village.

That first season was also enlightening for me because I discovered that I felt at home on the mound, that I belonged up there. Often I heard things while excavating or making my way through the plaza—voices, whispers, singing, and chanting. Sometimes I thought I saw someone in my peripheral vision, someone from the past. But although I felt something of the past, never did I feel any sense of an unsettled spirit world. I knew I would return.

And in May 2002 I did, after two more semesters at the University of Mississippi. There stood the mound, beckoning to me. What would it reveal this season?

On May 10, elders and tribal legislators from the Chickasaw Nation arrived to view the mound and the project. I was nervous, because not all elders approved of the excavations going on at Shiloh. But these visitors, I was pleased to see, grew excited about what we were finding. I spent much of the

Figure 16.3. Chickasaw officials, elders, and tribal legislators visiting the Shiloh excavations in 2002. The author stands fourth from left.

day with them and answered questions as best I could. There were many questions, because the mounds are part of our traditions, sacred, and to some a hope that oral traditions would be proved.

The crew spent May and much of June digging down through the temple mound's many layers. Often in Mississippian archaeological sites, excavators find the soil that makes up the mounds to be mottled, because the builders mixed together dirt of different colors, dug from different places. Not so in Shiloh's Mound A: each of its layers was a uniform red, white, or another shade created deliberately by mixing the two. Each time the mound was enlarged with a new layer, it was capped with red or white soil. People traveling the river by canoe would have seen either a red mound or a white mound—unvegetated, nothing like the grass-covered mounds we see today. Considering the traditional symbolism of

the two colors, perhaps the mound sent viewers a visual message that the town was at war or at peace. The mound was speaking! As a Chickasaw, I was thrilled to see two sacred colors brought to life on the mound over and over again.

Many house floors began to become evident as well. On August 6, while working on a house floor, I uncovered an unusual hearth. I had to sit for a moment and say a silent prayer. It was a moment that took my breath away and brought me face-to-face with the past in a way few people ever get to experience. The last person who sat at this hearth might well have been a woman a thousand years ago.

I had been taught that the Chickasaw woman was the guardian of the hearth, manager of the affairs of her home and family, mother and matriarch, head of her lineage. She built houses, planted and ground corn, and fed her family. Often she was

Figure 16.4. A chunkey stone found atop a buried summit of Shiloh Mound A.

excavation unit, my trowel struck the beautiful red clay floor of a house. Shelter is one of the most elementary requirements of humankind. For me this floor represented much the same thing the hearth had represented: family and the women of the house. The women maintained the house and kept its floor clean.

On July 22, Rena Duncan, the historic preservation officer for the Chickasaw Nation, visited the site. We spent a while discussing what this project meant for the nation and how so many aspects of it fit with what we believed to be true about Chickasaw culture in the past—the way the houses were constructed and their floors and hearths finished. The evidence matched up with what the Chickasaw were known to have been building in early historic times.

On August 14, as fellow archaeologist Susan Alt and I excavated another floor, we came upon charcoal, which turned out to contain broken pottery and twined cordage. This was another important moment for me as a Chickasaw. All the evidence so far had pointed to the same kinds of houses my ancestors had built historically, and now Susan and I had uncovered the same type of cordage Chickasaw people used to tie thatching and walls together. A find like this brought life to the people who resided at Shiloh in the past and made them real.

One day, as I sat near the edge of the mound above the Tennessee River, daydreaming about how the mound might have looked to people canoeing up and down the river, the *Delta Queen*, a sternwheel steamboat, dropped anchor and with whistles announced its arrival. I could easily imagine visitors hundreds of years ago beaching their canoes and, in much the same way, loudly announcing themselves and their friendly intentions.

On October 21, while working in a trench in Mound A, a crew member uncovered an intact chunkey stone. What a find! Chunkey was one of many games the Chickasaw played and continued to teach their children over time. It is difficult to explain the feeling I experienced—a feeling of life and excitement running through me—when I held

a healer and protector. And there I sat, next to a hearth where Native American women once sat. I felt life and power and recognized that I came from this. I was a strong woman from a long line of strong women. It seemed right that I sat there now.

Often during the summer, Native American people visited the site and paid their respects, wanting to know only that things were being handled respectfully. I was proud to tell them that they were. I was proud because the head archaeologists and crew were all working together and making great strides in the relationship between archaeologists and Native people, including the Chickasaw Nation.

Over the next winter, I went back to the mound three times. It was hard to stay away—it was as if the mound were calling me. I could scarcely wait until the next season, but at last, July 2003 rolled around. On my first day back, while opening an that chunkey stone in my hand, knowing that some of my ancestors had once competed with it. The chunkey stone was one more proof of a continuity that many people believe Native Americans have lost. On the same day, someone found a mussel shell with a hole drilled through it, the kind of shell from which Native people historically made beads and necklaces. One more tradition verified.

As the days passed from summer to fall, I watched for the same changes the people of Shiloh would have watched for—the changing colors of the trees, the flowering and dying away of plants, an increasing coolness in the air. People would have prepared for winter by collecting and storing food for the days they would spend inside, surrounded by family, passing on the stories of the culture. Every layer I helped removed from the mound represented, for me, the layers of the lives of the people of Shiloh. I would spend my winter telling of my time there.

I head west. The mound is closed and awaits the time when another group will be allowed to excavate. I have reconnected with my childhood passion, my wanting to know what it means to be me and where I came from by doing archaeology. Shiloh has answered many questions about the past and the people from whom I descend. I feel honored that the old ones spoke to me, allowed me a glimpse of the past, and gave me the many feelings I experienced.

April 24, 2005, 10:00 p.m. I have come from the west. I am not supposed to be here. I sit on the mound and listen to the past. But this time it includes the voices of people who lived here and the voices of the people I worked with for three summers. This time I look at the full moon and wonder, how many times did the old ones look at the moon and dream?

Donna J. Rausch was born in Texas in 1955 and lives in Ste. Genevieve, Missouri. A member of the Chickasaw Nation, she holds a master's degree in anthropology from the University of Mississippi. She is site director of the Felix Valle State Historic Site in Ste. Genevieve and teaches cultural anthropology online for Pulaski Technical College in Little Rock, Arkansas.

Figure 17.1. The Mississippian capital now known as Moundville, Alabama, looking south across Mound B (*foreground*) toward Mound A (*center*). The inset shows the full layout of the town's mounds.

The Rise and Demise of Mississippian Capitals in the Southeast

seventeen

Charles R. Cobb and Adam King

Mississippian towns embody a duality reminiscent of that in the medieval cities of Europe. One side of the coin is the repetitive, cookie-cutter configuration of the sacred precinct at the core of each community. All across Europe, cities such as Paris, Cologne, and Prague are instantly recognizable by their towering cathedrals and clusters of religious and royal buildings, from baptisteries to palaces, which defined their spiritual and political centers. Crowded around these zones sat bustling tenements and shops, full of people who could only imagine what life was like for the nobility and priests behind the imposing walls. Similarly, Mississippian capitals inevitably center on a large plaza ringed by earthen mounds that rise above the surrounding community. Powerful chiefs lived on the tops of some pyramids, temples surmounted others, and spreading out around the mound-and-plaza core stood houses filled with people who owed fealty to the leaders who overlooked them. This pattern repeated itself across the Southeast, whether the town now sits in Arkansas, North Carolina, or Alabama.

Just below the façade of sameness lies the other side of the split personality of medieval European and Mississippian towns: expressions of diversity that reflect narrowly local traditions. Cologne, Prague, and Paris in the 1200s might have shared ideals about the importance of monarchies as the bulwark of the political order and the pope as arbiter of religious belief, but they differed wildly in

languages, food preferences, and myriad other idiosyncrasies. The same was true in the American Southeast: the recurrence of mound-and-plaza architecture over a vast landscape masked a wealth of cultural diversity. Three particularly impressive sites—Moundville, now in Alabama, and Etowah and Ocmulgee, both in Georgia—well exemplify the two faces of southern Mississippian towns.

At its peak around 1250 CE, Moundville was a sprawl of neighborhoods and grand earthen mounds

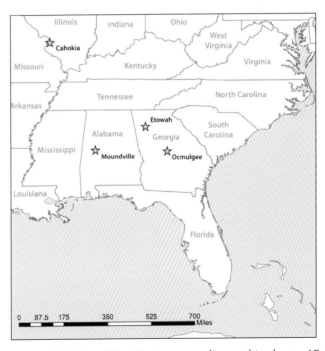

Figure 17.2. Major Mississippian towns discussed in chapter 17.

Figure 17.3. Stone palette from Moundville incised with a design depicting a rattlesnake.

surrounding an enormous plaza. Covering almost two hundred acres, the community encircled itself with a defensive wall, or palisade, of vertically set timbers studded about every hundred feet with a bastion, or projecting tower. Despite its size, Moundville may never have housed more than fifteen hundred residents. The scale of its building efforts might reflect the ability of Moundville's leaders to draw on labor pools from the nearby countryside. People probably flowed and ebbed through its gate as they came to work or take part in important religious and ceremonial events and then returned home to their villages.

Moundville's beginnings were modest. In 1120, it was just one of many southeastern villages where people were adopting new Mississippian traits such as maize farming, wall-trench houses, and shell-tempered pottery. Then, in the 1200s—for reasons unknown—the populace started building at an unprecedented scale, suddenly and quickly.

Still visible today are the mounds they erected encircling a plaza of about thirty acres—an area that could hold forty modern football fields. The main

platform mound, Mound B, overlooking the plaza from the north, stands more than fifty feet high. All the mounds show a regularity of placement and size that reflects considerable planning. For example, the alignment of mounds on the western side of the plaza seems to mirror that on the eastern side symmetrically. Large and small mounds alternate in pairs around the plaza. Some notion of social order and ranking seems to have shaped the town's configuration, such that the most powerful families lived on and around the largest mounds overlooking the plaza.

Moundville eventually became one of the largest Mississippian centers in the Southeast. As the town grew rapidly in the 1200s, its resident elites and artisans participated in the trade of a suite of exotic objects made from copper, marine shells, mica, and other valued materials. As part of their burial customs, Moundville people placed some of these objects in graves with their honored dead, persons who in life likely held some kind of elevated status. Prized items might be decorated with foreign symbols, their imagery similar to a style with origins in the greater Cahokia region in Illinois. Archaeologists find similarly decorated exotic goods at other Mississippian centers as well; perhaps they reflect Moundville's participation in a belief system that swept the Southeast at this time.

The zenith of Moundville's size and artistic accomplishments was also a time fraught with danger. Concerned about their safety, possibly from competing Mississippian centers, inhabitants built and several times rebuilt their protective palisade. Yet analyses of skeletal remains from Moundville demonstrate little trauma that can be attributed to warfare. It seems possible that the threat of conflict remained just that, and the sheer size of Moundville and its defensive works were enough to intimidate would-be attackers.

After a dynamic century of growth, at around 1300 the inhabitants of Moundville abruptly deserted their imposing capital. Although the reasons underlying their exodus are unknown, people who remained in surrounding communities continued to use the site for ritual purposes. Moundville effectively became a necropolis, a place to which people brought their dead for burial. The few residents who stayed appear to have been religious caretakers. Moundville lived on in its capacity as a sacred place for another century or so, until it fell into disuse by around 1450.

To the northeast of Moundville, its contemporary, Etowah (plate 17), was a sizable capital encompassing more than fifty acres. In its heyday in the 1300s, its leaders held sway over much of what is now northern Georgia and adjoining regions. Etowah's long and uneven history spanned more than five hundred years, from as early as 1050 until contact by Spanish explorers in the 1500s. During this time its residents constructed at least six platform mounds, multiple plazas, and a defensive palisade and surrounding ditch.

In its earliest manifestation, before 1300, Etowah seems to have been a town at peace, undefended by walls. Perhaps the very building of its first earthworks helped diffuse the threat of violence from neighbors by promoting group solidarity. Mississippian mounds were strongly symbolic and were constructed in stages. The placement of a new mantle of soil on each stage was a means of renewing the earth and its fertility, ensuring that crops matured and life went on in the community. Etowah's citizens regularly participated in feasts as part of the ceremonies surrounding mound building. They then threw the remains of their feasts—mainly food scraps and broken pots—into large pits left where workers had removed soil for mound construction. These communal renewal practices brought ethnic groups together from the surrounding countryside to create a new kind of community in northern Georgia.

The multiethnic character of early Etowah is suggested by pottery that appears to have come from different places, but it may be reflected most strikingly in details of community organization revealed by recent remote sensing surveys. This work has identified one hundred magnetic signatures below the ground surface that closely match the signatures of excavated Mississippian-period wall-trench structures—the earliest Mississippian architectural form at Etowah. These magnetic anomalies cluster around a series of small plazas, giving the appearance of discrete neighborhoods within the larger town. This pattern of subcommunities is what we might expect if Etowah were composed of distinct social segments.

By 1200 Etowah was a modest community organized around two platform mounds and a set of public buildings flanking a small central plaza. Not long afterward, residents mysteriously abandoned the town for decades. When people eventually returned around 1300, they transformed Etowah with massive mound-construction projects, the creation of a walled plaza, and ultimately the building of a surrounding fortification complex consisting of a wooden palisade and ditch. Houses again flanked the core of mounds, but the small, discrete neighborhoods of earlier times never recurred.

One new feature was a special mortuary mound, Mound C. Only a select segment of Etowah society received burial there, and many deceased elites went to their graves accompanied by elaborately crafted symbolic objects. Like similar objects found at Moundville, much of what was made and buried at Etowah was influenced by art styles and ideas from the Cahokia region, although executed in a local style.

Figure 17.4. Shell gorget from Etowah, carved in a local style called Hightower. The "birdman" figure, a hybrid of a warrior and a falcon, is common in the Southeast.

Etowah did not enjoy the same success as Moundville in fending off attackers. At its height, around 1375 CE, enemies burned its fortifications and desecrated its sacred mortuary temple. Again the populace left, and Etowah remained empty for almost a century before people returned. By that time, around 1500, another town had taken its place as the most important one in the region, and Etowah had become a peripheral center in Coosa, a large Native American polity that the Spanish explorer Hernando de Soto visited in 1540. Within a few decades of de Soto's visit, Etowah was abandoned for a final time as its inhabitants, ravaged by disease and social disruption, joined other groups and formed the nucleus of what would become the Creek Confederacy.

New Deal Archaeology

The Mississippian town of Ocmulgee was among the first sites to be tackled by one of the archaeological armies organized during the Great Depression, when New Deal work programs funded excavations throughout the Southeast. Often employing hundreds of unskilled workers at large sites under a handful of professional archaeologists, these projects saw an astounding amount of earth moved. Recognition of the importance of Ocmulgee led the U.S. Congress to declare it a national monument. Field and analytical methods refined there and at other sites in the 1930s exerted a lasting influence on archaeologists, and the enormous amount of data generated by New Deal excavations transformed our knowledge of the ancient Southeast.

Figure 17.5. New Deal archaeology crew excavating a prehistoric mound in Alabama.

Figure 17.6. Artist's reconstruction of Ocmulgee, showing the earth lodge, Mound D1, between the Great and Lesser Temple Mounds.

Ocmulgee, an enigmatic Mississippian town in present-day central Georgia, was one of the largest and earliest mound centers in the Deep South. Founded no later than 1100, Ocmulgee had a much shorter history than Etowah or Moundville, lasting for just a century or two. Eventually, the town covered some 170 acres and boasted eight mounds, including forty-five-foot-tall Mound A. Unlike at Etowah and Moundville, the architecture, pottery, and burial practices associated with Ocmulgee did not carry on or combine local traditions. Indeed, they are unlike anything found at contemporaneous sites in central Georgia. For this reason, researchers think Ocmulgee may represent an intrusion of foreign people and practices into the region.

We know that at Ocmulgee's founding, residents built two mounds—the Great and Lesser Temple Mounds—and a series of large, sequentially occupied public buildings at the southern end of the community. Among these early buildings were circular structures commonly called earth lodges, although these may never have been completely covered with earth like Native earth lodges of the Great Plains. The most famous example, the Mound

D1 Lodge, sat between the Great and Lesser Temple Mounds as part of the original ceremonial core. It measured forty feet in diameter, and the base of its wall was covered with banked earth. The shape and size of this building resemble those of southeastern Indian council houses in historic times—facilities in which community leaders met for ceremonial and political purposes. Presumably, then, Ocmulgee's earth lodge and mound complex formed the focal point of the town's civic and ceremonial life.

Later, the town grew to include two or possibly three additional mound-and-earth-lodge complexes. These were separated by open space that seems to have been left unoccupied or at least used sparingly, implying that the complexes were separate facilities for different social segments. In this way they are not unlike the paired mounds around the Moundville plaza and the small plaza groups at Etowah. Perhaps spatial arrangements accommodating distinct social groups were common elements in early Mississippian centers throughout the Southeast.

Later in Ocmulgee's history, its residents created a mortuary mound similar to Mound C at Etowah.

The Ocmulgee Earth Lodge

Lodge D1 at Ocmulgee National Monument is a remarkable public and ritual space, today reconstructed for visitors to enter. Its most intriguing feature is a raised clay platform shaped like a hawk or falcon with a two-pronged or forked-eye surround. This imagery resembles a Cahokian style and made its earliest appearance in the Deep South at Ocmulgee. The platform sits directly opposite the entrance of the earth lodge, facing east and the rising sun. A large hearth dominates the center of the lodge, and the circular perimeter is lined with prepared clay seats that grow progressively larger and more elevated as they approach the platform. The three seats on the platform itself are the highest in the lodge.

Figure 17.7. Reconstructed Lodge D1 at Ocmulgee. The reconstruction is completely covered with earth, but archaeologists now believe that only the bases of the walls were covered with banked sod.

Dubbed by archaeologists the Funeral Mound, it consisted of as many as seven construction stages and contained 150 human burials in its layers and nearby. Although most of the deceased were placed in simple pits, either unaccompanied by grave goods or at best ornamented with shell beads, several people received more elaborate treatment. This

included burial in log-lined tombs and interment with ornate artifacts, including effigy pottery, marine shell cups, native copper, and, in one case, a stone celt of a kind typical of the Cahokia region. This special mortuary treatment suggests that Ocmulgee society, like that at Moundville and Etowah, was socially ranked, so that some persons had special access to valued objects.

Ocmulgee ended as mysteriously as it began. By 1300, if not before, people abandoned the site forever. The unique material tradition created there disappeared from the central Georgia landscape, to be replaced by a way of life derived from Etowah to the north. Whether the people who built Ocmulgee left the region or somehow became part of the towns that grew out of its decline remains unknown.

Moundville, Etowah, and Ocmulgee shared a certain veneer of site planning, architecture, and social hierarchy. Their commonalities allow us to readily categorize them as belonging to a larger Mississippian phenomenon that in some way connected towns and villages over a large swath of the Southeast. Yet these three communities pursued divergent social, economic, and ceremonial lifeways, lending very different arcs to their histories. Whereas Moundville and Etowah were rooted in local traditions, the residents of Ocmulgee apparently immigrated into central Georgia. Etowah and Moundville had long occupational histories during which the communities were recast, sometimes more than once, but Ocmulgee's history was relatively brief. Etowah seems to have fallen to invaders at one time, whereas the other two towns apparently escaped serious conflict.

One of the more intriguing unanswered questions regarding the three towns is what relationship they bore to Cahokia, the colossus to the northwest. At Ocmulgee, excavators have found Cahokia-related objects and imagery, including the unusual celt found in Mound C and the raptorial bird artwork featured in artifacts of Cahokia-derived style. These objects hint that connections to Cahokia played a role in the founding of Ocmulgee; perhaps its pioneers were even Cahokian immigrants. At Etowah and Moundville, ritual objects associated with greater Cahokia's classic style appeared only after 1250 CE, by which time Cahokia had gone into decline and its former political and ritual power had waned. Yet the memory of Cahokia lived on through the spread of its ceremonial art to these new towns to the south.

Charles R. Cobb is a professor of anthropology and the director of the Institute of Archaeology and Anthropology at the University of South Carolina. Long interested in power and inequality among Mississippian societies, he most recently has explored warfare, health, and structural violence in the middle Cumberland region

of Tennessee. He is also studying southeastern American Indians during the colonial period, with a focus on the materiality of frontiers.

Adam King is a research associate professor in the South Carolina Institute of Archaeology and Anthropology and special projects archaeologist for the Savannah River Archaeological Research Program. Using archaeological excavation coupled with remote sensing and the study of ancient imagery, he researches the way Mississippian societies came into being and changed during their individual histories.

Suggested Reading

Drooker, Penelope B.
1992   *Mississippian Village Textiles at Wickliffe*. University of Alabama Press, Tuscaloosa.

Emerson, Thomas E.
1997   "Cahokia Elite Ideology and the Mississippian Cosmos." In *Cahokia: Ideology and Domination in the Mississippian World*, edited by Timothy R. Pauketat and Thomas E. Emerson, pp. 190–228. University of Nebraska Press, Lincoln.

Emerson, Thomas E., and R. B. Lewis, editors
1991   *Cahokia and the Hinterlands: Middle Mississippian Cultures of the Midwest*. University of Illinois Press, Urbana.

Fagan, Brian
2008   *The Great Warming: Climate Change and the Rise and Fall of Civilizations*. Bloomsbury Press, New York.

Fowler, Melvin L.
1997   *The Cahokia Atlas: A Historical Atlas of Cahokia Archaeology*. Illinois Transportation Archaeological Research Program, Studies in Archaeology, no. 2. University of Illinois, Urbana.

Fowler, Melvin L., Jerome Rose, Barbara Vander Leest, and Steven R. Ahler
1999   *The Mound 72 Area: Dedicated and Sacred Space in Early Cahokia*. Illinois State Museum, Reports of Investigations, no. 54. Illinois State Museum Society, Springfield.

Hally, David J.
1994   *Ocmulgee Archeology 1936–1986*. University of Georgia Press, Athens.

King, Adam
2003   *Etowah: The Political History of a Chiefdom Capital*. University of Alabama Press, Tuscaloosa.

Pauketat, Timothy R.
2009   "America's First Pastime: Did Rolling Stones Spread Mississippian Culture Across North America?" *Archaeology*, vol. 65, pp. 20–25.
2009   *Cahokia: Ancient America's Great City on the Mississippi*. Viking-Penguin Press, New York.

Picture Credits

Color section, after page 64. Plate 1, photo by Ira Block, used with permission of the National Geographic Society. Plates 2, 7, and 10, courtesy ISAS. Plate 3, artwork by Michael Hampshire, used with permission of Cahokia Mounds State Historic Site. Plate 4, photo by Walter Larrimore, courtesy National Museum of the American Indian, Smithsonian Institution. Plate 5, photo by T. Pauketat, used with permission of the St. Louis Art Museum. Plate 6, used with permission of the artist, Chloris Lowe Sr. Plate 8, photo by T. Pauketat, used with permission of Cahokia Mounds Interpretive Center and Western Illinois University. Plate 9, photo courtesy Cahokia Mounds State Historic Site. Plate 11, annotated LiDAR image by W. F. Romain from model data provided by Tom Emerson and Mike Farkas, courtesy ISAS. Plate 12, annotated LiDAR image by W. F. Romain from model data provided by Tom Emerson and Mike Farkas, courtesy ISAS. Plate 13, photos by Elsbeth Dowd, copyright Sam Noble Oklahoma Museum of Natural History, University of Oklahoma. Plate 14, photo by Linda Alexander, courtesy ISAS. Plate 15, individual photos by Linda Alexander and Kenneth Farnsworth, courtesy ISAS. Plate 16, individual photos by Kenneth Farnsworth, courtesy ISAS. Plate 17, © 2004 by Steven Patricia, used with permission of the Art Institute of Chicago; inset courtesy Adam King. Plate 18, used with permission of the Smithsonian Institution. Plate 19, courtesy National Park Service, Southeast Archeological Center. Plate 20, image courtesy of its creators, F. Limp, S. Winters, and A. Payne.

Front matter. Maps 1–3 by Timothy R. Pauketat.

Chapter 1. Fig. 1.1, mural by Lloyd K. Townsend, courtesy Cahokia Mounds State Historic Site. Figs. 1.2, 1.5, 1.6, and 1.8, photos by T. Pauketat. Fig. 1.3, photo by Tamira Brennan. Fig. 1.4, courtesy National Park Service, Shiloh National Military Park. Fig. 1.7, adapted from T. Pauketat, *Chiefdoms and Other Archaeological Delusions* (Walnut Canyon, CA: AltaMira Press, 2007). Fig. 1.9, photo by T. Pauketat, map drawn by and used with the permission of F. Terry Norris.

Chapter 2. Fig. 2.1, detail of scene 18 from "Panorama of the Monumental Grandeur of the Mississippi Valley," circa 1850, distemper on cotton muslin, Saint Louis Art Museum, Eliza McMillan Trust 34:1953, courtesy Saint Louis Art Museum. Fig. 2.2, map by Molly O'Halloran. Fig. 2.3, photo by Linda Alexander, courtesy ISAS. Fig. 2.4, drawing by Doug Kassabaum. Fig. 2.5, courtesy Division of Anthropology, American Museum of Natural History. Figs. 2.6 and 2.8, created by V. Steponaitis. Fig. 2.7, © Robert S. Peabody Museum of Archaeology, Phillips Academy, Andover, all rights reserved, used by permission.

Chapter 3. Figs. 3.1, 3.3, and 3.6, courtesy ISAS. Figs. 3.2 and 3.5, drawings by Glenn Baker. Figs. 3.4 and 3.9, maps by Molly O'Halloran. Fig. 3.7, map by Molly O'Halloran, adapted from Melvin Fowler, *The Cahokia Atlas: A Historical Atlas of Cahokia Archaeology* (Urbana: Illinois Transportation Archaeological Research Program, 1997). Fig. 3.8, used with permission of the British Museum. Fig. 3.10, base map courtesy ISAS. Figs. 3.11 and 3.12, photos by T. Pauketat.

Chapter 4. Fig. 4.1, photo by W. F. Romain. Figs. 4.2 and 4.4, drawings by W. F. Romain. Fig. 4.3, rows A and B, redrawn by W. F. Romain after illustrations in Timothy R. Pauketat and Thomas E. Emerson, "The Ideology of Authority and the Power of the Pot" (*American Anthropologist*, vol. 93, no. 4 [1991]: 919–941); Roberta J. Griffith, *Ramey Incised Pottery* (Urbana: ISAS, 1981); and George C. Dick, "Incised Pottery Decorations from Cahokia, a Middle Mississippi Site in Western Illinois" (*Missouri Archaeologist*, vol. 17, no. 4 [1955]: 36–48). Fig. 4.3, row C, redrawn by W. F. Romain from photographs published in Warren K. Moorehead, ed., *Etowah Papers* (New Haven, CT: Yale University Press, 1932); and Madeline Kneberg, "Engraved Shell Gorgets and Their Associations" (*Tennessee Archaeologist*, vol. 15, no. 1 [1959]: 1–39. Fig. 4.3, row D, left, redrawn by W. F. Romain from William H. Holmes, *Art in the Shell of Ancient Americans* (Washington, DC: Second Annual Report of the Bureau of American Ethnology, 1883); center, redrawn by W. F. Romain from Calvin S. Brown, *Archaeology of Mississippi* (Mississippi Geological Survey, University of Mississippi, 1926); right, redrawn by W. F. Romain from James A. Brown, *The Spiro Ceremonial Center* (Ann Arbor: Museum of Anthropology, University of Michigan, 1996). Fig. 4.5, map by Molly O'Halloran. Fig. 4.6, reproduced from Melvin L. Fowler et al., *The Mound 72 Area: Dedicated and Sacred Space in Early Cahokia* (Springfield: Illinois State Museum, 1999), courtesy Illinois State Museum. Fig. 4.7, drawing by Herb Roe. Fig. 4.8, contour map by Martha Ann Rolingson, annotated by W. F. Romain, reproduced from Martha Ann Rolingson, *Toltec Mounds: Archaeology of the Mound-and-Plaza Complex* (Fayetteville: Arkansas Archeological Survey, 2012), by permission of the Arkansas Archeological Survey.

Chapter 5. Fig. 5.1, photo by Lauren Murphy-Moore. Fig. 5.2, linework by Angela Collins, used with permission of Dale Henning, John Doershuk, and the Office of the State Archaeologist, Iowa City, Iowa.

Chapter 6. Figs. 6.1 and 6.2, engravings no. 21 and 22, respectively, from Theodor de Bry, *Grand Voyages*, 1591. Fig. 6.3, replica by Errett Callahan, photo by T. Pauketat. Fig. 6.4, drawing by A. VanDerwarker.

Chapter 7. Fig. 7.1, courtesy ISAS. Fig. 7.2, photo by Linda Alexander, courtesy ISAS. Fig. 7.3, photo by T. Emerson, used with permission of ISAS and the St. Louis Science Center. Fig. 7.4, painting by Lloyd K. Townsend, used with permission of Cahokia Mounds State Historic Site. Fig. 7.5, photo by Thomas Emerson, used with permission of ISAS and the Gilcrease Museum.

Chapter 8. Figs. 8.1, 8.4, and 8.6, photos by R. Boszhardt. Fig. 8.2, map by R. Boszhardt. Figs. 8.3 and 8.5, photos by T. Pauketat.

Chapter 9. Figs. 9.1 and 9.2, drawings by Bernard Perley, University of Wisconsin–Milwaukee. Fig. 9.3, photo by T. Zych, courtesy Milwaukee Public Museum; MPM catalog numbers, left to right, 714, 56653, 49783, 56849, 13339, 14820.

Chapter 10. Fig. 10.1, engraving no. 39 from Theodor de Bry, *Grand Voyages*, 1591. Figs. 10.2, 10.3, and 10.5, photos by S. Alt. Figs. 10.4, 10.7, and 10.8, courtesy North American Archaeology lab, University of Illinois. Fig. 10.6, reprinted from April K. Sievert and J. Daniel Rogers, *Artifacts* from the Craig Mound at Spiro, Oklahoma (Washington, DC: Smithsonian Institution Press, 2011), with permission of the Smithsonian Institution.

Chapter 11. Figs. 11.1 and 11.2, photos by T. Pauketat. Figs. 11.3, 11.4, and 11.5, reprinted from Staffan D. Peterson, "Townscape Archaeology at Angel Mounds, Indiana: Mississippian Spatiality and Community" (Ph.D. diss., Department of Anthropology, Indiana University, Bloomington, 2011). Fig. 11.6, image by S. Peterson.

Chapter 12. All illustrations by the authors.

Chapter 13. Fig. 13.1, photo by T. Pauketat, courtesy North American Archaeology lab, University of Illinois. Fig. 13.2, individual photos by Linda Alexander, Steven Boles, and Kenneth Farnsworth, courtesy ISAS. Fig. 13.3, created by Mera Hertel, courtesy ISAS. Fig. 13.4, created by Mera Hertel, adapted from a drawing by William Henry Holmes, *Handbook of Aboriginal American Antiquities, Part 1, Introductory, the Lithic Industries* (Washington, DC: Smithsonian Institution, 1919), courtesy ISAS. Fig. 13.5, photo by T. Pauketat. Fig. 13.6, individual photos by Kenneth Farnsworth, David Dye, and Missouri Archaeological Society, courtesy ISAS.

Chapter 14. Figs. 14.1, 14.3, and 14.6, courtesy Dickson Mounds Museum. Fig. 14.2, map by Molly O'Halloran. Fig. 14.4, courtesy ISAS. Fig. 14.5, courtesy Western Illinois University, Macomb.

Chapter 15. Fig. 15.1, courtesy Jeff Door and Robert Cook. Fig. 15.2, map by Robert Cook. Fig. 15.3, photo by Andrew Sawyer. Fig. 15.4, photo by Robert Cook.

Chapter 16. Figs. 16.1, 16.3, and 16.4, courtesy National Park Service, Southeast Archeological Center. Fig. 16.2, adapted from P. D. Welch, N. P. Hermann, and J. E. Cornelison Jr., "Mapping Procedures," in *Archaeological Investigations at Shiloh Indian Mounds National Historic Landmark (40HR7) 1999–2004*, eds. D. G. Anderson, J. E. Cornelison Jr., and S. C. Sherwood, pp. 208–224 (Tallahassee, FL: National Park Service, Southeast Archeological Center, 2013).

Chapter 17. Fig. 17.1, photo courtesy University of Alabama Museums, Tuscaloosa; inset courtesy Vernon James Knight Jr. Fig. 17.2, map by Charles R. Cobb. Figs. 17.3 and 17.5, courtesy University of Alabama Museums, Tuscaloosa. Fig. 17.4, courtesy David H. Dye. Fig. 17.6, reproduced from Charles H. Fairbanks, *Archeology of the Funeral Mound: Ocmulgee National Monument, Georgia* (Washington, DC: National Park Service, 1956; reprint, Tuscaloosa: University of Alabama Press, 2003). Fig. 17.7, courtesy Adam King.

Index

Numbers printed in *italics* refer to illustrations; numbers beginning with uppercase P refer to plates; numbers printed in **bold** refer to maps.

Aataentsic (Grandmother or Old Woman), 58
Algonkian mortuary temple, *26*
Alt, Susan M., 1–11, 27, 75–79, 115
Angel Mounds State Park, ix, 81, 82, 83–85; chunkey stones, 73; location, **viii**; pyramid mounds, *80*; site plan, **83**, **84**, **85**
Animal fibers, 76
Animals and priests, 59–60, *60*
Anthropomorphic art, scarcity of portable, 56
Archaeological sites: in central Illinois River valley, **100**; Mississippian, **xiii**; and Native Americans, 112–113; perishability of artifacts, 79; publicly accessible, viii, ix–xii
Architectural alignments and layouts: of Cahokia central precinct, 24, 25–26, 33–34, 36–38, *37*, 41n2, **P7**, **PP10–12**; of Cahokia East St. Louis compounds and neighborhoods, 23–24; and Coles Creek culture, 15; and Hopewell culture, 33, 37; of houses, 29, 84; of lunar shrine complexes, 29; Mesoamerican as prototype for, 4; of missions and shrines, 63; of outposts, 38–39, 65, 81–85, *82*, **83**, *84*, **118**, *118*, **119**, 119–125, *123*, *124*, **P17**; and Plum Bayou culture, *32*, 40; posts as precincts' organizational axes, 24; and religion, 30; separate mound-and-earth lodge complexes, 123, *123*
Arrowheads, 67, *67*
Azimuths, 33, 34, *34*, 36, *36*, 41nn1–2
Aztalan State Park, ix, *66*; artifacts, 69; burial garments, 78; chunkey stones at, 72; elite residences, 66; founded, 5; location, **viii**, **63**; violence at, 67, 69

Baires, Sarah E., 21–31
Baskets, 56, 76
BBB Motor site: goddess figurines, 37, 55–56, *56*, 57, 58, P14; lunar relationship to Monks Mound, *37*; temple complex, 58–60
Beakers, Caddoan, 14, *14*
Benden, Danielle M., 63–69
"Birdman" motif, 27, 122
Black color, symbolism of, 67
Black drink, 9, 14, 45, P2, P5
Blood Run National Historical Landmark, **viii**, ix, 44, *45*
Boszhardt, Robert F., 63–69
Brackenridge, Henry Marie, 21–22
Buckeye Bend site, 103, *103*
Burial practices. *See* Mortuary practices
Burrow pits, 25

C. H. Nash Museum, ix

Caddoan culture: Earth Mother associations, 58; languages, 4, 14; platform mounds arrangement, 15; relationship to Cahokia, **14**; Snake Woman, 56; transition to Caddoan-Mississippian, 5
Caddo-Mississippians, 4
Caddo Mounds State Historic Site, **viii**, ix
Caddo Nation, 14
Cahokia, **22**, **28**; axis mundi, 25, 33; Big Bang, 5; and Caddoan culture, 14; and central Illinois River valley, 101; and Cole Creek culture, 4; departure from, 10; and Etowah and Moundville, 121, 124–125; food needs of, 51; importance of, 11, 43; largest building in, 25; location, 22; modern destruction of, 22, 22–23; neighborhoods, 26, 28; and Omulgee, 124; outliers, **28**, 29–30; peak of power, 51; population, 4–5, 28, 40; role of, 9–10; size of, 21, 23, 51; taxation system, 51; Umoⁿhoⁿ oral history, 44. *See also* specific precincts
Cahokia central precinct, *xvi*, *21*, P1; alignment, 24, 25–26, 33–34, 36–38, 41n2, **P7**, **PP10–12**; current condition, 2; palisade defense, 30; pyramid clusters, **24**; Rattlesnake Causeway, 25–26, 33, 66, **P11**; size of, 93
Cahokia East St. Louis precinct, **22**, **23**; alignment of compounds and neighborhoods, 23–24; burials of women, 27; destruction of, 31; palisade defense, 30; population, 28; temple figurines, 58; violence at, 30–31
Cahokia Mounds State Historic Site, **viii**, ix
Cahokia St. Louis precinct, **22**, **28**
Causeways: from Monks Mound to Mound 66, 25–26, 33, 66, **P11**; purpose of, 28
Central Illinois River valley, 99–104, **100**
Ceremonial feasts: food and drink consumed, 9, P2, P5; location of, 17–18; and posts, 16, 17; for renewal, 121
Ceremonial weapons, 93, 96, *97*
Charnel houses, 26
Chert: blades, *51*, 64, 67, 97, PP15–16; quarries, **94**, 94–95, *95*; types of, 94, 95, 96, 108, PP15–16
Chickasaw Nation, 111–112, *113*, 113–114, *115*
Chipping method of toolmaking, 93, 95
Chucalissa, **viii**, ix
Chunkey, 57, *57*, 64, *70*, 71–73, *72*, *73*, *115*, 115–116, P9
Chunk-yards, 71, *72*
City of the Sun, 33
Climate, 2, 10, 104
Cloth and clothing, *75*, 75–79, *76*, *78*, *79*, P18
Cobb, Charles R., 119–125
Coles Creek culture, 4, **13**; architectural layouts, 15; ceremonial posts, 9; Feltus Mounds site, *12*, **15**, 15–18, *16*, *17*; human sacrifice, 9; language, 4; and maize, 13, 53; and Mississippian culture, 5, 13; platform mounds, 4, 15; pottery, *16*, 17, 67; religion, 18
Color, use of, 67, 113